Re-Imagine Your Life

Re-Imagine Your Life

SEVEN SECRETS TO ACHIEVE YOUR DREAMS

ROSA YORDAN

Publishing Company

New York

Copyright © 2015 by Rosa Yordan

All rights reserved. Printed in the United States of America. No part of this book may be used, reproduced, distributed, or transmitted in any form or by any means, or stored in a database or retrieval system, without the prior written permission of the publisher. For information, address Transformation+ Publisher, 76 North Village Avenue, Rockville Centre, New York 11570.

Library of Congress Control Number: 2015909716

ISBN-13: 978-0-578-16531-8

ISBN-10: 0-578-16531-7

Transformation+ books may be purchased for educational, business or sales promotional use. For information, contact us at www.transformationplusinc.com

Every effort has been made to ensure that the information contained in this book is accurate. It is published with the understanding that the publisher or author is not rendering legal, accounting, financial or other professional advice. Also the publisher or author is not rendering personal relationships and other self-improvement advice. If self improvement or professional advice is required, the services of a certified professional should be sought. As each person is unique, the questions specific to each person should be addressed to an appropriate professional. The ideas, procedures and suggestions contained in this book are not intended as a substitute for consulting with your physician and other specialists. All matters regarding health, finances, relationships, etc, require the supervision of specialists. Neither the author nor the publisher shall be liable for any loss, injury, or damage allegedly arising from any information or suggestion in this book.

Contents

Preface: "Living Life" by Bonnie Mohr 9
Acknowledgements 10
Introduction 11
Dream Big 13
Tools Needed for Your Journey 14

Part 1: Revealing The Seven Secrets to Achieve Your Dreams ... 15
    Secret # 1: How to Identify Your Strengths 17
    Secret # 2: How to Survey Your Life's Problems 22
    How to Evaluate Your Self-discovery Checks 36
    Secret # 3: Discover How to Envision Your Dreams 45
    Secret # 4: How to Create Your Goals 56
    Secret # 5: How to Generate a Plan 60
    Secret # 6: Discover How to Timeline Your Tasks 73
    Secret # 7: You Have Arrived! Now Live Your Dreams! 79

Part 2: How to Apply The Seven Secrets to Relationships 85
   Secret# 1: How to Identify Your Strengths 88
   Secret# 2: How to Survey Your Life's Problems 91
   Secret# 3: Discover How to Envision Your Dreams 107
   Secret# 4: How to Create Your Goals 111
   Secret# 5: How to Generate a Plan 115
   Secret# 6: Discover How to Timeline Your Tasks 140
   Secret# 7: You Have Arrived! Now Live Your Dreams! 145

Part 3: How To Apply The Seven Secrets to Careers 151
   Secret# 1: How to Identify Your Strengths 154
   Secret# 2: How to Survey Your Life's Problems 157
   Secret# 3: Discover How to Envision Your Dreams 165
   Secret# 4: How to Create Your Goals 168
   Secret# 5: How to Generate a Plan 171
   Secret# 6: Discover How to Timeline Your Tasks 181
   Secret# 7: You Have Arrived! Now Live Your Dreams! 187

Part 4: Bonus: Especially For Older Adults 193
A Final Word 208
About The Author 209

Preface

I went to a friend's house and saw the following verse on a plaque that was mounted on her living room wall. When I read it, I was in awe. This verse spoke about everything I have written in this book; the journey, the dreams, the love, the Lord, longevity...

LIVING LIFE

"Life is not a race — but a journey. Be honest. Work hard. Be choosy.

Say "thank you", "I love you" and "great job" to someone each day. Go to church, take time for prayer. The Lord giveth and the Lord taketh. Let the handshake mean more than pen and paper.

Love your life and what you've been given, it is not accidental — search for your purpose and do it as best you can. Dreaming does matter. It allows you to become that which you aspire to be.

Laugh often. Appreciate the little things in life and enjoy them. Some of the best things in life really are free.

Do not worry, less wrinkles are more becoming. Forgive, it frees the soul. Take time for yourself- plan for longevity. Recognize the special people you've been blessed to know.

Live for the day, enjoy the moment."

Bonnie L. Mohr

Acknowledgments

I wish to thank people who have been supportive of me. I thank my parents who sparked values in me and were my heroes; my sisters with whom I shared many life experiences; my children from whom I learned the importance of being an adult and parent; my grandchildren who bring me so much joy; my friends who listened and spoke with me about fun-filled times and life problems; the men whom I received and expressed love and affection to; my professors and mentors who inspired me; my bosses who allowed me to implement my ideas at the workplace; and God who has granted me so many wonderful experiences.

A special thanks to V. Porter and S. Grimes for their editorial suggestions; and Kiran for book cover suggestions.

Special thanks to Jewel Tiffany, J. Bayfield, my grandson, Erik John Jr. and Liza Yordan

Living Life verse, Bonnie Mohr Studio. Images and website copyright 1997-2013. Bonnie Mohr Studio. All Rights Reserved. 10454 160th Street, PO Box 32 Glencoe, MN 55336, 1(320) 864-6642 (800) 864-6642, www.bonniemohr.com

Quote by Mark Twain "The Equalizer" movie 2014

Introduction

Before we begin I must reveal that this interactive self improvement book focuses on relationships and careers, and contains a bonus section for older adults. Please position yourself in a relaxing environment, and while reading this book, be prepared to be engaged. I am unbiased - someone you can connect with and receive support from. I will offer ideas. If you feel these ideas will be helpful, by all means, use them. However, I strongly suggest that you read my contact information at the end of the book for one-on-one consultations or group workshops. Please keep this in mind: you may have to consult with your doctor or other specialists; especially if you plan to make use of some of the suggested ideas.

This interactive book is divided into four parts. Each of the four parts contains worksheets within the book. The worksheets consist of activities that can assist you in obtaining a clearer picture of your vision. You can record past and present experiences and feelings. Also you can record how you plan to make progress while on your journey to success. In addition, you can use your worksheets as a reminder of a past challenge that has now become your own personal success story.

Since the book is divided into several parts, you can choose to read the entire book or the specific topic(s) that are relevant to you. However, Part 1 of the book, *"Revealing the Seven Secrets to Achieve Your Dreams,"* is the prequel to all of the other sections. In Part 1, you will receive keys to unlock secrets that will help you while you are on your quest to become successful in your personal and professional endeavors. Also you will acquire suggestions and/or methods as to how you can reduce your weight, manage children with behavioral issues and manage your own stress.

So it is highly recommended that you read Part 1, then any or all other parts of the book. Part 2 of this book focuses exclusively on *"Applying the Seven Secrets to Relationships."* Relationships can involve a significant other, family member or friend. Part 3 spotlights *"Applying the Seven Secrets to Careers."* The Bonus section, or Part 4, *"Especially For Older Adults"* is for older adults or others who want to encourage elderly people to live a more active life, as well as motivate seniors to accomplish those dreams which they still manifest in their hearts. If you are not an older adult, you may want to read this section to gain some insight as to what you would like to do now as well as in your future. Regardless of whichever parts of the book you read — know that you are not alone.

Partner, I will share stories, some of which may cause you to say to yourself, "that seems like a challenge I am experiencing right now!" Or you may say, "I would love to accomplish what that person has accomplished." All of these stories, suggestions, requested responses and power breaks are to assist you in your journey of self discovery, and ultimately help you acquire your personal and professional successes.

Dream Big!

Let's begin the journey. I have four questions I want to ask you. When was the last time you felt fulfilled? When was the last time you accomplished something? Have you had a dream since childhood that you have not yet accomplished? And my last question is, if you were to *re-imagine your life*, what would your life look like? I want you to ponder for a moment before giving a response to these four questions.

As your life coach and partner I will guide you through your journey of self discovery. Together we will focus on your strengths, your life's problems and how to get those successes you want using your God-given tools and my *"Seven Secrets to Achieve Your Dreams."*

The *"Seven Secrets to Achieve Your Dreams"* is designed to help you meet your challenges and to lift you up so you can achieve your goals. Partner, we are going to have to break through some of those barriers you have developed since childhood. So be prepared to express and experience all kinds of emotions. How else can you become successful?

Don't worry! During our times together we will focus solely on you. Isn't it great to have a partner devoted to helping you accomplish your goals, your dreams? I will be your motivator and partner throughout this journey. I know how important it is to have someone cheering for you and supporting you. Together we can make your dreams become a reality. We have a wonderful journey ahead of us. Are you ready to begin? Are you ready to gain the keys to unlock the *Seven Secrets to Achieve Your Dreams*? This is going to be a great partnership — a terrific one!

Tools Needed For Your Journey

What is needed for this journey? Since you will be asked to think, envision, write responses and look back at what you wrote, you will need a pen or pencil. If you have a small picture of yourself as a teenager and another picture of yourself as an adult, that would be wonderful!

At times I will encourage you to take a "power break." Power breaks consist of taking deep breaths, drinking a cup of hot, minty, herbal tea or a cool glass of water, standing up and stretching out your back, neck, arms and legs. You may want to consider lighting an aromatic candle.

Occasionally I will ask you to close your eyes and smile. Let me say this to you, when we probe into those unpleasant topics about your life, I would like you to feel as comfortable as possible. Since you have a goal to fulfill I am offering these tools along with my support to help you through your transformation stages.

Are you ready to learn the seven secrets to empower yourself and make your dreams come true? Are you truly ready to unleash your greatness from within? Fantastic!

Part 1

Revealing the Seven Secrets to Achieve Your Dreams

The two most important days of your life are the day you were born and the day you find out why.

Mark Twain

The Seven Secrets Revealed

Many people talk about what they could have or should have done to make their lives better. Have you asked yourself any of these questions lately: How can I turn my life around? How can I have a better life? As you gain access to each of the Seven Secrets, you will acquire a method to help you do exactly that - turn your life around so that it will be wonderful. I will guide you along the way. Please remember to bring along your personal tools. Expect to rediscover some of your own personal secrets and to face some challenges. Then again, as you make use of the Seven Secrets, plan to make some new remarkable self discoveries.

Are you ready to attain your seven keys and capture the secrets that will yield success? Fantastic!

Partner, it's time to turn your first key.

Secret # 1:
How to Identify Your Strengths

Now is the time to obtain the first key that will unlock the "Seven Secrets to Achieve Your Dreams." Once again, are you charged up? I know I am. Let's begin our journey.

Your first key will unlock the first Secret which is to "Identify Your Strengths." What positive attributes do you have? When people compliment you, what do they tend to say? Are you hardworking, friendly, responsible, or self motivated? Or do any of the following characteristics fit you: ambitious, an achiever, an action taker?

I want to share a story about a woman I coached, whose strengths allowed her to meet her career challenge. She felt uncomfortable and wasn't sure if she was ready to make a career change after more than a decade working for her present company. She felt unfortunate because her position had been eliminated, and initially she doubted her ability to take on a different type of job. She asked me to give her guidance. However, before we continued she had to decide if she preferred to leave the company or pursue the new position offered to her at the same company. She decided that her goal was to acquire professional success, and opt for the new position at her present job site. Her big challenge was that she was unfamiliar with the tasks and duties of the new position.

We began working closely together. We probed deeply into her childhood and adult strengths as well as how she was able to obtain and successfully manage herself in her past position. Through her journey of self discovery, we began to identify and take notice of the strengths she had, such as determination and the ability to take action when necessary. Those were some of the positive characteristics that helped her to overcome her fears and stressors.

Under my guidance, she envisioned her goals, created a timeline and we also did some role-playing. These are some of the things that led to her success. In a short period of time, she learned the new skills at her new job and enjoyed her work. The greatest benefit was the fact that she became very much respected by her peers, co-workers and family.

There is something I need to add to this story, which could also happen in your case. There were some people who felt she should have given up and found a less challenging job elsewhere. However, because of the support she received from her boss and others, she achieved her goal because she was determined and not afraid to take action.

As you move along in your quest you will run into people who will support you, and others who may advise you to give up. Be thankful of your supporters. Now, years later, I have seen her work through several challenges with no thought of giving up. She is one of the most determined action takers I have met.

You are probably wondering why we are focusing on your strengths. Well, the simplest way to answer this question is to say that your strengths are the key to help you achieve your success. For instance, if you are a motivated and determined person, we can use those strengths to move you in a timely manner so that you can achieve your goals. Your strengths become your tools to help you meet your personal challenges, thus creating your own positive outcome. Furthermore, your strengths can help you come up with solutions to work through the problems in your own life. Partner, do you sometimes hear little voices saying, "Give up. Don't give up." Your strengths can give you the courage and desire needed to continue your journey so you will not give up on your positive endeavors.

Since part of your discovery of self is to recapture your greatness, I would like you to write responses pertaining to your positive characteristics on the "*My Strengths*" worksheet that follows. On the worksheet there are two sections. They are the "*Young Me*" and the "*Adult Me*" sections. I will be giving you directions on how to fill out the chart. In addition I will ask you several questions to help spark you with ideas and responses.

Let's refer to the "Young Me" side of the page. Place the picture of your young self on the top left side of the paper, above the "Young Me" section. Please do not attach the pictures to the page because you will reuse these same pictures again in other sections.

I want you to think about yourself when you were young. You have a youthful picture in front of you to help you to reminisce. Please write your positive attributes as a youngster; let's say up to age 18. For example, were you popular, friendly, caring, sharing, determined, responsible, self motivated, talented or helpful? The strengths you had when you were young helped you through many phases of your growth and development. Think about it. Most of your learning happened before you were eighteen. Your positive characteristics helped you to survive, and played a major role in your adulthood. Role models were most prevalent in your childhood, adolescent, and teen years. They could have been parents, teachers, clergy, extended family or an occasional stranger. Please write your positive characteristics on the left side of the page.

Now that you have focused on yourself when you were young, it is time to concentrate on you as an adult. Let's begin by placing the adult picture of you above the adult section. Now you probably know what I am going to ask you to do; write the positive attributes you have as an adult. Many of the positive characteristics you had as a child tend to continue into adulthood. As life happens we may change. Or life can add newer positive traits because you have gained more experiences and learned along the way how to meet your challenges. Look at your adult picture as you think. Record your thoughts on the right side of the page.

My Strengths

Young Me	Adult Me

Are you ready for the next step? I want you to review the youth and adult sections. Is there anything you would like to add to either of the two sections? Do you notice whether some of your characteristics are similar, or have new ones developed as you have become older? Or did some of your former characteristics vanish when you became an adult? And answer this question: do you want to get back a strength you once had? Just take a moment to think about yourself and process the 'you' of yesteryear and the 'you' of today. Think about your positive qualities. Admire them! Accept them! They are what makes you, you.

While working to create a positive outcome, be prepared to experience a newer and better you. Before we move to the next Secret maybe you have something else you would like to add to any of the columns. Keep in mind that you may want to look back at this section, especially if you need a positive boost, so do not leave out any of your great characteristics. When you complete your self-discovery assessments that will appear later in this book, and your assessment results are not at optimum level, I will suggest that you revisit the "My Strengths" worksheet you just wrote.

Secret # 2:
How to Survey Your Life's Problems

Now that we have spent time focusing on your strengths it's time to use the key to unlock Secret # 2, "Surveying Your Life's Problems." Thinking about your life's problems can be painful. It can cause stress and anxieties. In order to move towards your goals, it is wise to confront and conquer your fears and problems.

These life problems are holding you back from becoming your best and achieving your goals. You may become stressed, second-guess yourself, or may just want to give up. Some people experience plenty of problems in their lifetime and have difficulty seeing a way out of their situations. Therefore their life's problems will seem compounded. Some people become so stressed because they do not know how to start to tackle their problems. Others may feel too embarrassed to inquire about help. Then we have another group who just prefer to settle for what life is offering them at the moment, just barely living one day at a time. Do you find yourself falling into any of these categories sometimes, or often?

There are people who become addicted to something such as drinking, sex and non-prescribed drugs. Others become abusive. They may use verbal, emotional, physical or any combination of abuse towards family, friends and/or strangers. We also know that some people prefer to inflict self-pain. The last group of people I must include are the ones who have withdrawn themselves from society. They are so quiet. Many times no one pays them any attention because they are not disturbing or harming anyone else. Do you fit into any of these categories?

If you do fall into any of these categories, it is great that you are reaching out for help. It is fantastic that you want to achieve success and are ready to take the journey to make your goals become a reality; and you are now ready to uplift yourself. That is fantastic! Partner, depending upon your severity, I may recommend that you also seek more intensive interventions from a specialist.

I want to get a little personal. People complain about their hair, lips, nose, buttocks, chest, legs, eyes, weight, etc. Some people do nothing about it, others change their appearance. Have you dyed your hair, had plastic surgery, lost weight, etc.? Are you happy with the results? If that has helped to boost your self- image, and confidence — great!

There are other types of problems we can face. People experience problems in their interactions with others. I will share two stories of how interactions with others can present a major problem. The first story involves a parent and child. The second story concerns a woman and her relationship with co-workers and her bosses. Are you having either of these types of experiences?

Parents and guardians raising school-aged children can have their share of life's problems. Usually they have to deal with discipline issues. Are you a parent who has an elementary school child who is not acting appropriately and you want to do something about it? Do you feel especially embarrassed and not in control of your child when you pick your child up from the school playground?

Or are you experiencing the following kind of problem: after years of persevering, you finally pass mandated exams that qualify you for professional positions with a good salary and excellent benefits. However, you have been waiting several years at your current job for someone to hire you for one of the higher level positions. In the meantime, you notice that several other people are offered the position you desire. Also, you are bullied by co-workers, and your boss shows little respect towards you. Instead of the boss offering you a position, he has relocated you to another site. At the new site you are experiencing similar unpleasant situations such as lack of respect, and no one is offering you a position you are more qualified for.

Are you having either of these types of unpleasant experiences? Let's put these negative experiences on the table. Please do not consider withdrawing as an option. I am offering suggestions at the end of this Secret as to how you can handle the parent's dilemma, and also suggestions regarding the woman's problem of facing a career advancement dilemma.

Surveying your life's problems is designed to help you acknowledge your problems so that you can ultimately address them, challenge them, and finally get rid of them. If you do not take on these problems, you may wind up stuck in the same vicious cycle of accomplishing little or nothing.

When you have turned your life's problems around, then you can continue to have a healthy mind, body and soul. Therefore you can strive for some of the more wonderful things life has to offer. You are probably saying, "Rosa, that's easier said than done." Well, my response to you is that you already have two things in your favor. Number one, you are reading this book, therefore you are interested in empowering yourself and achieving your dreams. And my second response is that you are about to admit or already did admit to your life's problems, which is not something pleasant to think about.

So let's get started. We are going to refer to the *"Life's Problems"* worksheet so you can answer these and other questions. Have a pen or pencil available. Take the youthful picture of yourself and place it above the *"Young Me"* section. Then place the adult picture of yourself above the *"Adult Me"* section.

Life's Problems

Young Me	Adult Me

Secret # 2: How to Survey Your Life's Problems

I want you to stop for just a moment and take a power break. Let's take a few deep breaths. Deep breath, inhale; now exhale. Once again inhale, now exhale. If you want to sip your beverage this may be a good time. Now, let's get serious.

Are you ready to think about your challenges? Great! Right now I want you to think about your youthful days, up to age 18. What are some of the life problems that you experienced? Did you have problems staying on task? Were you ill most of the time? Did you have friends? Were you bullied, ridiculed or ostracized? We hear the term "bullied" mentioned more in the present day. However, I remember when I was a preteen some of my friends were bullied. Some peers even tried to bully me. I had to fight them off.

Now, take the time to write down your childhood problems on the "*Young Me*" section of the page. You may want to take a few more deep breaths as you write about your negative experiences. Since you have an aromatic candle, you might as well enjoy the scent of it.

Let's move to the "*Adult Me*" side of the page; because now it is time to focus on your life's problems as an adult. Are you experiencing difficulties in areas such as finance, relationships or health? Are you bullied or treated disrespectfully by friends, family or co-workers? Do you feel others are receiving what you think you should be entitled to, or are other people holding you back from your dreams? Do you feel you lack motivation or the ability to stay focused? Are you a procrastinator? Do you often feel embarrassed or too stressed to know how to tackle a problem? Are you barely living? Do you relate to any of the stories that were mentioned previously in this chapter? Once again, what are some of your life's problems? Take a moment to think about them and jot down your responses on the worksheet.

Remember what we did when we reviewed your childhood and adult responses in the "My Strengths" section? One thing I asked you to do was to note whether the adult and childhood strengths were the same. Now compare and contrast your life's problems. On your life's problems worksheet do you notice the same types of problems occurring over and over again? Or do you see a change? Do some of your problems you had in the past not exist anymore? Just review this section for a few more moments.

As your partner I want you to feel uplifted. Feeling uplifted will allow you to focus on what you can do. We will work to minimize or get rid of the negative energy that may be consuming you and eliminate obstacles that hinder your success.

I stated earlier that I would offer career advancement and parenting suggestions that relate to the two stories I mentioned previously. You can also go to www.transformationplus.com to obtain 4 ways to minimize fear.

CAREER ADVANCEMENT SUGGESTIONS

It is obvious that the woman mentioned earlier in this chapter wants to advance her career. It seems she may have problems with other professionals; her co-workers are bullying her, and the boss moves her to another site. In addition, the new boss does not seem to respect her.

If you are experiencing something similar, I want to start by asking you a few questions. What do you say when you are in a professional meeting? Are you quiet at meetings and give minimal responses or do you say too much? How do people react towards you when you say something to them? When people ask you questions do you respond with strong opinions or do you give no opinions? How are other people treated by co-workers and bosses? Who is treated differently? If other co-workers are treated similarly to you, what do all of you have in common? How are you different from the one who receives preferential treatment? Do you hand in your work on time or late? Are you a hard worker? Do you stay later to do exceptional work? Do you leave immediately when the work day is over? Do you spend time socializing with co-workers? Do you listen to criticism or do you criticize others?

I want you to try to understand why certain people are given preferential treatment. I have a few questions that delve into your childhood. Were you bullied when you were a child? If the answer is yes, how did you handle it? Did your parents take care of all of your problems when you were a child, and at your present adult stage of life?

I have a few suggestions. In order for you to advance in your career you may need to change your approach towards other professionals. Therefore my first suggestion is to make observations at work. Note how people who get what they want are treated, and how those who do not get what they want are treated. Second, observe what the accepted ones are doing in order to gain recognition. Observe how they are presenting their materials. Observe how they interact with their peers. I want you to notice that observation is the key to this beginning process.

The next phase is to find a role model. Decide who you would want to be your role model. Find out if this person, who is respected and has a position similar to the one you desire, would like to take you under their wings. Learn from the role model and ask questions. This is how you can become a better candidate for a more prestigious position.

We do not want you to ask your mentor to ask the boss to offer you a job. You can, but you need to first understand how to handle your own situations and learn a thing or two from the role model. What could happen is that you are offered a position but lose it immediately because you have not obtained the skills for maintaining yourself in the professional world. This would probably lead back to the disrespect and bullying situations. In the meantime, you can mimic your mentor in terms of how he/she handles professional obligations, then ask your mentor questions to clarify how and why that particular approach was used. Your mentor and you can do some role-playing of job-related scenarios. This could help you conquer some of the undue stress you are experiencing from co-workers who bully you, and bosses who show minimal respect towards you. Having a role model should help you stay focused on gaining respect at your job.

You should also want to demonstrate confidence and a positive self image. I want to address the topic of appearance. Dress code is important, especially when you are striving for a higher paying prestigious position. In the case of the woman I mentioned earlier, who was seeking a higher level position, wearing jeans to work daily was not to her advantage.

Partner, if you are experiencing this type of problem in your life, I strongly suggest you read *"Applying the Seven Secrets to Career Advancement"* Part 3 of this book. The information, exercises and worksheets are designed to focus exclusively on helping you with career challenges you may be facing.

BEHAVIOR MANAGEMENT SUGGESTIONS FOR PARENTS

Now let's move on to suggestions for parents who have children with behavioral issues. For reading purposes let's refer to this child as a male. This is the situation. You call your child, because it is time to go home; he chooses to ignore you, and runs away while you are trying to grab him to go home. You find yourself yelling and feeling angry and embarrassed because he does not want to listen. You notice that your child seems to be the least cooperative child in the school yard. Other parents at the school playground show empathy towards you because you do not seem in control of the situation. You want your child to pay attention to you when you call his name. I suggest that you create a plan with your child; then get feedback from him.

Here are two possible plans you may want to consider: "nip it in the bud" and "be consistent." These plans have worked extremely well for me and countless others, which is why I am sharing these approaches with you. Both plans require some work on your part. These plans allow the child to understand what is being asked of him. Please keep in mind that it may take some time for your child to change the behavior. So be patient. These plans minimize the friction between the adult and the child. The end results will be favorable for both you and your child. You may want to consider using both of these strategies if your child is acting inappropriately. In severe cases, such as hyperactivity, consult a doctor.

Regardless of which of the two approaches you decide to use, first you should have a calm, conversation with your child. Ask your child questions such as: how does he feel when you are yelling and grabbing him when it is time to leave the playground? Wait for a response. Respond to his feelings. Your child may state that it is not such a good experience; and he does not like that feeling. Then you can express how you feel. For example, you can say that you feel embarrassed, angry and you do not like nor want to feel that way. If your child did not respond initially, you can express your feelings first. Afterwards you can ask for his response again. Let your child know you want him to have fun with his school friends, but you also want him to come to you when called. Then ask your child if he would like to make a plan so that both of you can feel happy. Compliment your child for listening and responding to you.

Let's begin with the "nip it in the bud" approach. How does the "nip it in the bud" strategy work? This plan requires you to respond immediately to a situation that is inappropriate. For instance, if you want the child to come to you immediately, do not call him five or ten times. Take him home if he does not respond to you immediately. If you have repeatedly called your child in the past, I am going to say this to you — your child does not feel any need for change.

Here is a suggested solution to the problem. First let your child know you came up with a plan that will make both of you happy. The plan is for him to come to you when you call him. He will have ten minutes play time then he will be called to come to you. If he comes by the second call he can play some more. If he does not come by the second call he will be taken home. Let the child know the night before that both of you are going to begin the plan. As a reminder tell him in the morning that when you pick him up from school you will allow him to play outside for ten minutes. After ten minutes, you will call him to come to you.

Tell your child what you will say to him. At home you can role play the scenario. For example, if the child's name is Tom you can say, "Come here, Tom." Then say to Tom, "If you come to me by the second call you can continue to play." Let him repeat what you said to him. Then tell him when you see him after school, you will say the plan again, "Come here, Tom." This time he must respond by coming to you. If you role play this at home and give him a treat when he responds quickly and responsibly, the chances of success will be great and will occur soon. Then let him know this is how you always want him to react when he is at the school playground. Ask him if he has any questions, then respond to any questions he has.

Remind your child of the plan in the morning. When you see him after school the following day, say the "Come to me when called" statement again to your child as a reminder and then ask him to repeat it. Then say to him, "Great! I know you know what to do. Your good behavior is going to make both of us happy. Now go and play." Next, give him ten minutes of play time. Go close enough to him so that your child can hear you call his name. Call your child in an even tone; I mean a tone that is firm yet softly spoken. Wait and watch his response. Observe if your child looks at you, or acts like he does not hear you. If your child does not follow your direction, move a little closer so you know he can hear you the second time. Repeat the statement using the same tone. Wait and observe again. If all is well and your child comes immediately, tell your child his reward is more time to play. You can say, "You did a great job. I am so proud of you. Go play some more. Be prepared for me to call you again." If you want to give the child a treat when it is time to leave the playground that is fine. However, his main reward is the fact he earned extra play time. When both of you arrive at home, remind your child that tomorrow you will expect the same great behavior. Both of you will do the same thing again. You must repeat the rules at night and in the morning. Also, the child must repeat them to you as well.

However, if he does not follow the rules, take him home immediately. Chances are your child will probably continue the inappropriate behavior he was doing before. You need to explain to your child that both of you spoke about it at night, in the morning, and just before play time. In addition, he repeated the rules. Therefore, no play time for him! Then add that if he wants to play outside longer with his friends tomorrow he must do what he said he would do; and that is come to you immediately. This can be stated in a calm yet firm voice.

If this plan does not work after day two you can calmly ask your child why he does not come to you when you call him. Try to get an answer. Then you can ask him if he prefers not to play after school, because he seems to have difficulty coming to you when you call him. Wait and listen to his response. Ask him if he would prefer to come when you call him or go straight home. If he says he is going to respond to your call, review the rules again. If he says he prefers to go home, ask him why. He may not respond. Or something may be going on that needs to be addressed. Either way I suggest that you take your child home for a few days, and find out why he responded the way he did. If a situation or problem has occurred you may want to handle that first - for example he may have had a problem with a classmate who is bothering him and he does not want to be in the school yard while the other child is there. After the situation is taken care of then revisit the rules for "nipping it in the bud."

Let the child know he has choices; and those choices will give him either fun time or more time at home. This is how you can "nip it in the bud." You are handling a situation based on what is occurring. Under no circumstances should you approach your child by using verbal or physical abuse. This can cause a conflict situation. We do not want children to have negative, abusive experiences. So please do not act abusively because once we cool off, we begin to feel ashamed or remorseful and realize we lost control. This may cause the original problem to never be fixed.

"Be Consistent" is another approach you can use when handling children who do not cooperate. This approach is not as easy as one may think. I will explain why; it is so easy to say one thing then do something else. For example, if you told the same child, Tom, that he must respond to you by the second call, and you continue to call him four more times, then we have a problem. The rule was that he must respond by the second time. I highly suggest that you take him home because he did not listen. Also, if he came to you the first time as required and then he responded to you on the fifth call later that day; that is a no-no. You stated the rules; then you did not live up to your part of the bargain. Therefore the child is confused and has no need to do as you say.

I have seen parents get angry at children. They wonder why their child doesn't listen to them. In many cases the parent was not consistent. A child who does not want to obey the rules is glad to have a parent who is inconsistent. If you are a parent or guardian who identifies with this situation, then "nip it in the bud" and "be consistent" may be just the answer for you. In terms of behavior, a general rule is that it takes about three weeks for a person to change their behavior. Let's try to change it in less time.

After a week of the same positive behavioral results, I encourage you to get feedback from the child. You can ask your child questions such as how does he feel when you do not yell at him; and does he feel both of you need to continue to state the plan each day and night? Also ask him if he feels he can come to you by the second call without any reminders. If the response is yes to the latter question, try it and see what happens. If all is well then you have changed your interaction with your child. Keep in mind that each situation is different — such as your relationship with the child and how you interact with him.

Partner, before you consider engaging in either of these approaches, you may want to turn them into a game. Let's call it a "happy" game. You can let your child know you will place a "happy face" sticker on his hand and yours when he comes immediately to you. This will be proof that both of you are happy. Isn't this the objective? Now, if you want a more detailed rewards system, you can create a "happy" chart. This can also be a nice way to bond with your child. Each time your child is given a sticker he earns two points, which represents both his and your stickers. Either of you can put check marks on the "happy" chart for the amount of points he earned each day. At the end of the week reward him with something special, but please allow him to make a mistake, because we know no one is perfect!

Managing your child's behavior is important. I want to end this segment by asking parents and educators of toddlers and school-aged children these two questions: does your child/student know that he can obtain whatever he wants by acting out, yelling, crying or having a temper tantrum? Do you feel it is easier for you to give him whatever he wants so that he will cease his inappropriate behavior? Be honest. If you answered yes to either of these questions, we need to talk.

Children need nurturing and adult guidance. We have to praise children when they act appropriately and when they do the right thing. We also need to guide them as to how they should interact with us and others. Ultimately we want our children, as well as ourselves, to have as many positive experiences as possible. For 7 ways to manage your child go to www.transformationplus.com.

SELF-DISCOVERY CHECKPOINT:

It is time for a Self-discovery Check. Several of these checkpoints will occur throughout the book to keep you focused on your goals and to monitor your progress. Also, with your recorded responses you can review what you have written and take note whether your mind, actions or feelings have remained the same or if they have shifted. If change has occurred, you will probably be able to pinpoint when the change occurred.

I would like you to refer to the *"How to Evaluate the Self-discovery Check"* that follows, to gain a better understanding of each diagram, how to score your responses and how to evaluate your results. In addition, you will learn when it is recommended to proceed to the next chapter. Also there are suggestions to help uplift you and possibly change your stress levels, if necessary.

How to Evaluate Your Self-discovery Checks

During the time we spend together you will be asked to do "self-discovery checks." This will allow you to discover how you are feeling at that particular time. While you are on your journey, you may experience some ups and downs. Your energy level may be lower during some points and higher at others. Your stress level may be higher at different times during your journey. You may feel more successful and energetic during certain stages of your transformation. Remember, we want you to become successful in your personal and professional endeavors. Therefore you will be asked to answer the self-discovery questions very truthfully.

How will you be able to tell if you are ready to continue your personal journey? At the end of some of the Secrets there will be a "Self-discovery Check." You will be asked to answer questions about your energy level and whether or not you feel stressed. You may want to refer back to this section of the book to assess your scores. After you acknowledge your stress level and energy level scores, you will know when it is best to advance to the next Secret.

If your results are very good, you should continue. This means your results indicate your stress level is low and your energy level is high. In other words, you feel eager enough to take on your challenges and continue your journey towards success.

However, if your stress level is high and your energy level is low, it is not recommended that you move on to the next Secret. Partner, if you are not feeling at ease, and you are feeling out of sorts, truly this is not a good time to pursue your dreams, at least, not at that moment. Do not be surprised if you find yourself feeling stressed at some point or another during your journey. Don't worry, it will be okay. We will try to find ways to get you to a positive state of mind. Actually I will offer you suggestions.

SCORING PROCESS

Stress Number Line: So how can you evaluate your self-discovery readings? Using the *"Stress Number Line"*, which is numbered from one through ten, your stress level results should fall below level 3. This means you have minimal stress. If you are at level 3 you have some stress yet it is not consuming you. Therefore if you score 3 or less, you can move on to the next Secret.

However, if your stress level indicates higher than level 3 you are experiencing stress. I highly suggest that you do something that will help you feel positive. High stress levels are not what you need to acquire success. Above all, be honest with yourself in your answers, to get the proper benefit from this journey. Let's look at the "Stress Number Line" to become familiar with this assessment.

Stress Number Line

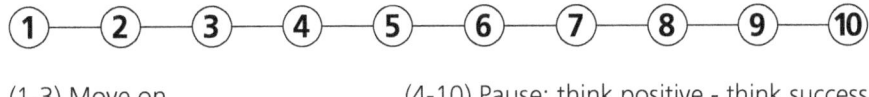

(1-3) Move on   (4-10) Pause: think positive - think success

Stress vs. Success Balance Beams: How do you evaluate yourself using the *Stress vs. Success balance beams*? The next chart consists of three types of balance beams. If you choose the diagram on the right side of the page with success at the top; your balance beam illustrates you have a positive attitude. This is indicated by the letter "b," "I can succeed/ Success is possible." In this case you can continue your journey because you feel self confident. Therefore the balance beam which indicates "I can succeed/ Success is possible" should be tipping very close to the top, near the success mark or at its highest point. When you have positive energy and feel you can be successful, then you are ready to move forward.

What does it mean if you choose the balanced scale? The balanced scale indicates that you feel balanced, as noted by the letter "c." This is acceptable. However, I want you to notice that I used the word 'acceptable.' We are striving for 'exceptional.' In order to accomplish something you cannot be at a mediocre level. You have to reach high, dig deep into the pit of your body, soul and mind because you want to make a significant change in your life. If the change was so simple and required little or nothing from you, wouldn't you have done it already? So once again feeling balanced is okay, but feeling great, energetic and charged up is what is needed to achieve your dreams. Since the balance beam indicated by the letter "c" is acceptable, you can move on.

Now let's look at the balance beam that shows stress is higher than success/joy, as illustrated on the balance beam on the left side of the page. This states "stress is overpowering," which is indicated by the letter "a." This indicates you should pause. You are not ready to move on yet.

Part 1. Revealing the Seven Secrets to Achieve Your Dreams

Energy Level Number Line: Now let's engage in an Energy Level check. I want you to be aware of your efforts. I want to make sure you are concentrating your energies on the task at hand. This is another indicator as to whether you are ready to engage in the next task.

As you look at the *"Energy Level Number Line"* that follows, you will notice the numbers range from 1 through 10 (1 = low energy, 10 = high energy). If your energy level is in the 7-10 range, then you are considered to have a high energy score. What does a high energy score mean? It means you are motivated, charged up, ready and able to take action. You can concentrate your energies on the task at hand and make a forceful effort. With high energy results you are ready to move on to the next Secret.

However if your energy level ranges between 1- 6, you need to pause. Why? Because you do not feel you can make a vigorous effort to continue your journey. Even though you may think you are capable or want to continue the process, something may hold you back.

Energy Level Number Line

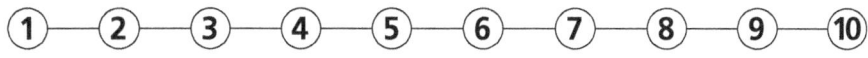

(1-6) Pause: think positive - think success   (7-10) Move on

Supportive Suggestions: If your "self-discovery" results are not at the optimum level, we have to get you to change your mindset to a more positive one. You have goals and ambitions. Aren't you dreaming big? So try your best to act it and feel it so that you can achieve it.

Here are some suggestions you may want to consider. Partner, first begin by thinking you can have it all! You can have the money, house, car, the high-level position, the relationship, the family and the fit body — whatever your heart desires. It is all within your reach. So act as though you are capable of doing what you set out to do. If you need to—STOP. Ponder on some positive thoughts. Think of something great you did. Think of someone who did something nice for you. Think of the wonderful thing you are about to accomplish. If you need to, listen to a favorite song, listen to a comedian or read an inspirational quote. Or maybe you need some quiet relaxation time. You know what makes you feel serene. Do what is necessary, so you can continue your journey. Maybe you will need to refer to your "*My Strengths*" worksheet, and read the positive statements you wrote about yourself out loud. Please do something immediately.

If you believe in God, I suggest you should have conversations with Him. You can ask God for help and guidance. Ask Him to put you on the right path. Who knows, the correct path may be greater than you imagined. While you are alone, be still and listen.

If you think you need to, spend time alone by yourself, maybe a day or two would be sufficient. You may want to do some moaning, crying, thinking and whatever else is needed to get to the surface any negative feelings that are stored up. Then allow the feelings to escape. Yes, let those unpleasant feelings escape from your mind, body and soul. The purpose of being by yourself is so that you will not be able to verbally or physically harm others. Also, you do not need others around to give you empathy or suggestions all the time. Take some time to self reflect. I do suggest that you let those close to you know you need some quality time for yourself. For three reasons: first, so that your loved ones will not feel you are neglecting them; second, so they do not have to feel concerned about your wellbeing; and third, let them know you can be a better person when you feel you are ready to interact with them again. Remember, you are responsible for your own thoughts and actions.

Why am I asking you to self reflect? Because you need to be concerned about what is going on around you as well as within yourself. It's important to clear your own mind and soul when you feel troubled. Then you can move on with your life and accomplish the great things you desire. Remember — you are wonderful!

If you find yourself unable to get out of your present emotional state, you may need to consult with a professional for help. That's okay! If something triggered you to discover a deep issue you had in the past, it's time to address it. You do not want deep-rooted issues holding you back from accomplishing successes. Try to remember that you are operating from a paradigm of hope. Hope that your dreams will become a reality. Hope, which means you can have it all! Also, remember you have a coach to guide you. You are not alone.

The key to your success is to think positively, positively, positively! When you feel you have a positive frame of mind, then you should retake the Self-discovery Check. If you score better than on the previous test that is great. If not, you need to continue your journey on another day. Partner, you have to be motivated, concentrate and give more than one hundred percent in order for your visions to become realities. When you have the acceptable scores you are a step closer to accomplishing your wonderful dreams.

Now is a great time to take your first Self-discovery Check. So far, we have focused on your strengths as well as your life's problems. Let's find out how you are feeling right now. Remember, we want you to become more successful in your personal and professional life so answer the questions truthfully.

STRESS LEVEL ASSESSMENT

1. What is your present stress level from 1 through 10? Please circle your response.

(1 = very low stress level, 5 = some stress, 10 = very high stress level).

Stress Number Line

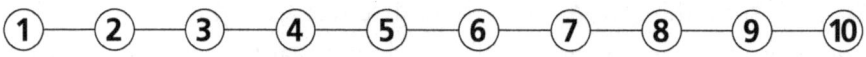

2. What stresses are you experiencing right now, if any? Explain.

3. **Based on the Stress vs. Success balance beams that follow:**

    i. Which of the 3 diagrams best represents you?

      a. Stress is overpowering (you feel unable to handle your stress)

      b. I can succeed/ Success is possible (you can control it and feel more success than stress)

      c. Balanced (you feel some stress, but hope is in sight)

    ii. Which diagram best describes how you feel when you are involved with others on a personal or professional basis?

      a. Stress is overpowering

      b. I can succeed/ Success is possible

      c. Balanced

Stress vs. Success

Stress is over powering (a)

or

I can succeed/ Success is possible (b)

Balanced (c)

How to Evaluate Your Self-discovery Checks

4. **Do you feel you can achieve success in the near future?**
   Yes ___ No ___

   i. If yes, in what ways do you feel you can be successful?

   ii. If no, why not?

5. **How would you rank your energy level on a scale of 1 through 10? Please circle your response.**

   (1= very low, 5= some energy, 10= very high)

   Energy Level Number Line

   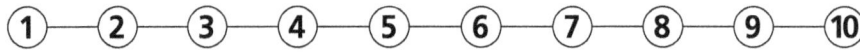

Secret # 3:
Discover How to Envision Your Dreams

We identified strengths and surveyed your life's problems and did the "Self-discovery Check." The key to unlock Secret # 3 is to *"Envision Your Dreams"*. What do I mean by envisioning your dreams? People tend to have dreams or thoughts of something or someone they are interested in. However they have not pursued that thought or vision yet. In other words, you have dreams of yourself doing or having whatever you are dreaming of. The following questions can help to spark some of those thoughts and dreams you may have had in the past. In the past did you have a vision? Did you achieve your dream? If yes, what led you to want to make that change in your life?

At a young age I learned that when you are determined and an action-taker then you can achieve what you envision. However you must have the vision first. Some of you may have had a similar experience to the one I am about to share with you. Others may have experienced more severe or less stressful situations that led you to want to change your circumstances. Or maybe your vision was not based on any type of stressful situation. My goal is to make you aware of the significance of visions. Visions can wake you up, get you motivated and guide you. Let's call your visions - dreams of what you hope to accomplish.

I am going to share a story about a married couple with children who demonstrated how significant a vision can be. Have you had this type of experience? This couple had a vision; and you will see how they went about achieving their dream.

So let's focus on this married couple's visions. The husband's first vision was to possess his own business. He accomplished his dream with the support of his wife. He obtained the required documents and certifications to own a business, even though he had limited English skills. That was a big accomplishment for him and the family. The business was quite successful.

One vision was achieved. What was the next dream, and why? They were happy tenants living on the twelfth floor in a Bronx apartment building. It seemed safe enough for the twelfth floor tenants to have their doors open. On rainy and snowy days all of the children who lived on the same floor roller skated and played board games in the hallway. Afterward, all of the parents cleaned up to make sure the hallway was neat and spotless. Several years later the couple decided they should move to a two-story apartment in the same complex with more bedrooms.

What led to their new vision? They moved without knowledge of their soon-to-be neighbors. Several years prior to the family moving into the two-story apartment, one of the neighbor's sons tried to bully the married couple's oldest daughter. Shortly after moving into the two story building the couple began to realize they lived amongst people who had been imprisoned, shot, etc. The married couple and their children's living experience were unpleasant and unsafe. Fear of gun shots and constant fighting in the building gave the family sleepless nights. Fortunately no one bothered the couple's family.

The husband and wife's vision was for the family to live in a safe environment; and to own a home with plenty of rooms, a backyard and a basement for entertainment. Based on their negative exposures and unsafe environment, the couple felt an urgent need to move as quickly as possible. The husband worked two additional part time jobs. The wife began to earn money by taking on a part time job when the children were at school and worked at their business on weekends. They did not splurge on expensive clothing or items. They stuck to the necessities.

Their vision became a reality. After working extra jobs, saving enough money, sticking to the plan and praying, the time came. The whole family went house hunting. The couple ultimately picked the house of their dreams. Shortly after, they were in their new, beautiful home in a safe environment. They did it! They achieved their dreams. This married couple had a vision, made a plan and stuck to it. They were my role models. Dreams do come true.

How important are visions? Are you clear about what you want to achieve? I want to spend some more time trying to help you to understand your ultimate vision. Why? Because vision is a vital ingredient you will need in order to gain success. Your vision will show you your end zone. When teaching peewees how to play softball, you need to take them by the hand and run with them to each of the bases: first, second, third, then home base. However you must also let the children know that they must run to home plate in order to gain points and possibly win the game. Therefore children playing softball know what is required of them, and the victory that comes when they make it to home plate. They envision themselves gliding towards home plate and team mates slapping them a high five.

Do you have a vision of retiring within five years? Do you see yourself going to pension consultations, speaking with financial advisors and recently retired co-workers in the near future? Do you envision yourself working extra hours at your present job or at another business so that you can earn enough money for fun-filled retirement activities very soon? Can you imagine yourself enjoying your retirement lifestyle; going places and doing things that make you happy? This type of retirement vision can lead to the sort of plans that need to be made sooner rather than later.

Envisioning one's dreams is not usually a one-dimensional path. A dream can take you in several directions. A more specific vision can usually move you through the process sooner and smoother than a broad, vague vision. However, there are exceptions.

Envision this — you want to purchase a car. You see yourself getting out of the driver's seat of a brand new car that is American made. The car is a red sports car with all of the upgrades. Your journey does not entail much work in order to find the car that you envisioned. You need the money, of course, and will probably go to at least one American car dealer looking for that special sports car. After all the paperwork is done, you have the brand new car that you envisioned. The goal of purchasing a car seemed to go smoothly.

However, if the car dealer does not have the color of the car you envision you have to make a decision. You can accept a different color, go to another dealership, find out if they can order it within your time span and wait for the car to come into the dealership. Or maybe you will decide to have the car painted. This path is not as smooth as the prior one. However, all in all this vision would not take long to obtain because you know what you want, even if it involves you making some minor changes or waiting a little while longer to acquire it.

What about a career vision? First of all it does not always matter whether you are young or mature in age and are seeking a career or career change. Regardless, this journey can consist of several paths. You may have one vision in mind and along the way you may have some positive and negative experiences which can put you on a new and improved path. The most important thing is that your outcome is favorable.

In your vision, are you passionate about the work you do or are you working just to pay the bills? I believe you want to do something enjoyable and satisfying in your life. Some jobs require many hours at work, such as owning a store that is open for 24 hours. Other jobs are nine-to-five office jobs. There are jobs that offer overtime, great pensions, bonuses and plenty of vacation days. Some jobs require uniforms, formal, or professional attire. Other jobs prefer you to dress casual. You may even be at home in your pajamas working on a laptop or computer. What do you envision? What you think, feel and do will ultimately give you the success you dearly want. As your coach I can envision this and role play scenarios to help guide you towards your specific path.

Typical careers that have been around for a long time and which just about everyone has encountered are doctors and teachers.

I am going to focus on doctors. Is this a career vision you want to pursue? If yes, these are some of the types of questions you can answer. What type of doctor do you want to be? For example: a surgeon, a pediatrician? Where do you envision yourself practicing - in your home town or in an underdeveloped country? These are just two examples of locations you may choose. Do you see yourself wearing a doctor uniform? Do you see yourself servicing patients, or teaching other doctors in your profession? Why do you have visions of yourself as a doctor? Is it because one of your siblings became ill at birth and you developed a strong desire and passion to cure children as a surgeon or as a pediatrician?

I have other types of questions on the topic of medical careers. Do you know any professionals in the field you wish to pursue? Have you spent time in a hospital learning and shadowing others? Do you have any physicians in your family? Do you watch videos and read educational literature to learn about the medical field? Do you feel you have what it takes to sustain yourself in this career? For example, let's say you have a vision of yourself as a surgeon. Are you okay with cutting into someone's body and seeing lots of blood? If you get light-headed when you see blood, I am not sure you should become

Secret # 3: Discover How to Envision Your Dreams

a surgeon. Although I received a scholarship to become a doctor, I personally did not pursue it mainly because of the blood.

Do you see yourself around children who are ill? If you do not like to hear children crying, especially during their immunizations, I do not know if you have what it takes to become a pediatrician. Also, I would like to think that pediatricians, who work exclusively with children, actually like children.

Your response to each of the questions can lead to other paths. One person may feel compelled to be a pediatrician in an underdeveloped country, while another may choose to be a surgeon who would like to teach other doctors to become surgeons at a teaching hospital. In these two images of a physician, the paths are different. Each doctor may require different contacts and mentors in order to obtain his or her vision. The types of diseases treated may differ based on the area where one works, so each doctor must be prepared for these undertakings. So where do you envision yourself working?

Let's talk about people with innovative visions. Several of their visions may need to be tested and tried before the public can reap the benefits. Two of the careers that fall into this category are scientists and game show creators. I know these two professions are extremely different; one group can save lives, while the other provides entertainment. Do you see yourself in the creative zone? Are you okay with trials and errors, and seeking new ideas and solutions? It is a wonderful thing when you have success with new ideas and solutions. However, how would you handle your failures and errors? You have to expect things will not always go right on the first trial. However the accomplishments are rewarding.

Does your vision entail you owning your own business? After you have observed businesses that are similar to the type you want —

envision you at your own business. What does it look like? Where are you located? What are you and your staff members engaged in? How are your customers responding to your services or merchandise? Think of how you are spending most of your time and energy. Contemplate your future profits.

If you love styling people's hair - what career vision do you have? Is it to work at a hair salon, or own your own salon? Or is your vision to work at a movie set styling a performer's hair?

I want to share a brief story with you. I remember one movie premiere I attended. There was a long line of women waiting to use the restroom. A female agent walked up to a woman and asked the woman standing nearby if she was interested in appearing in a movie? She responded by saying "yes" so the agent gave the woman her contact information. I wonder — did the woman envision herself as an actress? Nonetheless, everyone in the ladies room — including the woman — was shocked. So it does happen. Opportunity can exist when you least expect it. The woman was at a movie event, dressed like a celebrity, and landed an opportunity to appear in a movie. Location, location, location, plays a big role in achieving your goals. You have to be present in order to win 'it' at least in most cases. I just want to add - I are not sure the woman who received the offer had a vision of herself as an actress. However, the agent had a vision. Her vision must have been to find a potential actress. And she did.

Go to www.transformationplus.com to obtain 6 tips for a happier life.

Secret # 3: Discover How to Envision Your Dreams

A GUIDE TO FILLING OUT WORKSHEETS BASED ON A SPECIFIC VISION

The following section is a guide that will be used throughout Secrets 3 through 6. You will see how this person's vision evolves from a thought to a reality.

I am offering you a guide to help you fill out the following worksheet based on a specific vision. A man has a vision to own his own business. I will use this same vision throughout each of the Secrets that follow. Here is an example of how the Secret # 3 worksheet can be filled out. You may differ in your ideas and approach, and that is okay. However, this sample serves as a general guide. When filling out your vision please consider adding as many details as possible.

Secret # 3: My Vision

I see myself at a bakery store, wearing a baker's hat and white apron. I see other people working along side of me in my small shop wearing their aprons and hats with smiles on their faces. Yes, this is my shop. I can smell the sweet aroma of cakes, pies and cookies. I see the flour, dough and fruits such as strawberries and blueberries. I just finished preparing a cake and I am now presenting it to a customer. My customers are happy and have a smile on their face when they pick up their pastry we made for their special occasions. I am especially happy when my customers come back to my store and say they truly enjoyed the pastries we baked. My small shop is located in my neighborhood. Many of my customers know me.

Now let's focus on your vision. On the *"My Vision"* worksheet page that follows, you can place a small picture of yourself as an adult at the top of the page. At the bottom of the page you probably noticed six 'value' words. The six words are: career, family, health, integrity, relationships, and spirituality. These words can help clarify what you may be yearning for in your life right now. Look over these value words very carefully. Now list them by number in terms of their importance to you. Number one ranks as the most important, and number six is of the least importance to you at this time in your life. Please spend time prioritizing the six words.

I want you to bring the thoughts, dreams and visions you have in your mind to the surface. Now let's begin to envision something you want. *Re-imagine your life*. When I envision something, I always smile. Try to put a smile on your face as you envision your dreams. I would like you to take some deep breaths. Inhale, now exhale. Once again breathe in and breathe out. Envision yourself in a specific place, doing a specific activity. Who is with you? Or are you alone in this ideal setting? Visualize and imagine yourself. You are very happy, pleased with what you have accomplished. People have complimented you on how well you are managing yourself. You are living your best life and you feel uplifted. You have succeeded in reaching your goals and you feel wonderful.

Now that you have read what I suggested for you to imagine, breathe in and breathe out. Once again breathe in and breathe out. This time you can close your eyes and have fun envisioning. When you are finished with those wonderful images, open your eyes. This is probably the perfect time for you to write your vision on your "*My Vision*" worksheet page. You can start by writing or completing the following term: "I see myself ..." Or if you are artistic you may want to draw the images.

My Vision

Value words:
Career, Family, Health, Integrity, Relationships, Spirituality

_____	_____	_____	_____	_____	_____
1	2	3	4	5	6

Part 1. Revealing the Seven Secrets to Achieve Your Dreams

Let's review the chart. Are your priorities coinciding with your dreams? Did you already accomplish what you prioritized as number one? If not, is that one of your visions? Answering these questions can help you create clearer goals for yourself. Take this time to ponder and review the "My Vision" page again.

When we have discovered what is truly important to you via your imagination, we know the direction to take. Then we will know the type of goals which will be best for you. Your strengths will be the tools we can use to make your journey possible, and I will offer total support and guidance along the way. Since making these dreams a reality is important to you, I am sure you will work wholeheartedly to accomplish them.

Partner, you have just explored what is important to you. I hope you enjoyed this secret and feel uplifted and inspired. Since you have envisioned your dreams and written them down, you are ready to advance to the next Secret.

Secret # 4: How to Create Your Goals

You are probably feeling uplifted after envisioning your dreams and learning how other people have envisioned their dreams and achieved success. Are you ready to create your own goals? *"Creating Your Goals"* is the key to unlock Secret # 4. I want to define goals as those things you want to accomplish. The things you are aiming for in your life - your hopes, your aspirations. Is your goal to marry your partner, own your own business or travel around the world? So let's begin by deciding which goals are important to you and will give you satisfying results. Let's create goals based on what you envisioned and wrote on your "My Vision" worksheet. For example, was a vision you wrote about to own a chain of restaurants? If that is the case, some of your goals may be to learn how to manage your time and money, and speak with other people who own chains of restaurants.

Which of those visions you wrote about would you like to create goals for? Do you want to choose the vision that you feel will take the least amount of time to conquer, therefore giving you success in the shortest period of time? Or would you prefer to take on your visions in sequential order - the one which is the most important first, then your second most important vision second? If a large sum of money is needed in order to accomplish your vision, when will you attempt to make that dream your reality? Each vision you select can now become the goal you will be working to achieve.

In addition you may want to consider what type of work you need to put into the goal in order for you to be successful. Do you feel you have the mindset, time and energy to make that goal a reality? And are the people who you want to be a part of this goal available?

I would like you to spend some time thinking about your response to these questions and any other thoughts that may come to mind. Remember, you will be devoting plenty of time to these goals. You want to achieve these goals in order to create your new reality.

Actually, I have a few thoughts I would like to elaborate on before you make your final decision. My first thought is that you may want to consider choosing a goal you feel you can achieve faster. Why? Because this would enable you to quickly achieve your first taste of success. You would feel great, and more energized and ready to take on the next goal. And even more important, you would have acquired more 'strengths' such as being an achiever. Surely this can help you delve into your next challenge. In other words, you can use many of the strategies and strengths you acquired from your first goal to later work on more challenging goals. By taking this path, you could reflect on the positives and learn from any mistakes. Your positive experience will become one of your greatest assets as you approach your next challenge. In addition, you will develop self-confidence.

Now, if you decide to begin with the goal which is of the most importance to you, one advantage is that you have tackled your main goal immediately. You want to go for it. You are eager to make your dream become a reality, and feel you have what it takes to do just that — make it happen.

Each goal requires much from your mind, body and soul. You must commit yourself to do it. For example, would you feel better working to improve family ties or career advancement at this particular time in your life? Do you feel you are ready to create harmony with your loved one? These are the types of decisions you have to make. As you are thinking of at least four goals I want to ask you a few more questions. Are these goals realistic? Do you feel you will be able to reach your goals? Remember I am your partner. I will guide you through your goal reaching process.

Secret # 4: How to Create Your Goals

A GUIDE TO FILLING OUT WORKSHEETS BASED ON A SPECIFIC VISION

In Secret # 3, there was a guide to help you fill out the "My Vision" worksheet based on a specific vision. You filled out your vision worksheet in Secret # 3, after reviewing the sample guide. Now I will continue to give you a sample of how to decide on your goals based on a man's specific vision. Remember I am guiding you through a process. If you are considering owning a business you may differ in your approach. That's okay. My objective is to walk you through a process from a vision to creating goals stage. The following is a reminder of a man's vision to own his own bakery.

Secret # 3: My Vision

I see myself at a bakery store, wearing a baker's hat and white apron. I see other people working along side of me in my small shop wearing their aprons and hats with smiles on their faces. Yes, this is my shop. I can smell the sweet aroma of cakes, pies and cookies. I see the flour, dough and fruits such as strawberries and blueberries. I just finished preparing a cake and I am now presenting it to a customer. My customers are happy and have a smile on their face when they pick up their pastry we made for their special occasions. I am especially happy when my customers come back to my store and say they truly enjoyed the pastries we baked. My small shop is located in my neighborhood. Many of my customers know me.

Now let's look at one goal based on this man's vision.

Secret # 4: My Goals

My goal is to own a bakery shop. Why? I have dreamed often about it. When I bake pastries many people have complimented me and even asked me if I considered starting my own business. I have saved the money so this is a good time.

Write some goals you wish to achieve on the "*My Goals*" page. Please write about four goals and why you are choosing these goals. When filling out your goals please consider adding as many details as possible. Have fun writing your goals.

My Goals

① _____

Why?

② _____

Why?

③ _____

Why?

④ _____

Why?

⑤ _____

Why?

Secret # 4: How to Create Your Goals

Secret # 5: How to Generate a Plan

Let's take a brief power break. Right now I want you to take some deep breaths. Inhale, now exhale. Again inhale, and exhale. I would like you to follow this with a few soft breaths. This may also be a good time to just sit there and enjoy the relaxing aroma of your candle. In addition, you may want to enjoy a few sips of a soothing cup of herbal tea or a cool glass of water. If you want to stand up and stretch for a moment, do so.

Since you have decided which goals you want to achieve, it is time to pick up the key to unlock Secret # 5, *"Generate a Plan"* in order to reach your goals. You are probably wondering why we took a power break right now. Partner, the planning stage may take a while to develop. You have to plan the type of action you are willing to take in order to achieve your dreams; so you need to have a clear head in order for you to create a plan. You must decide on the approach you will use to make your goals become a reality - how you will go about getting what you want.

You must come up with a plan. The more detailed the plan is, the better the results. We both know we cannot simply say, "This is what I want," or, "I want to be a billionaire by tomorrow" — and presto — like magic, it happens. That's a fantasy! We have to be realistic. Becoming a millionaire may be your goal but you need to create a plan to make it a reality. For example your plan may be to read the stock market statistics daily and learn how to invest your money, if you want to become a millionaire. Or if your goal is to develop your public speaking skills then a plan could be to find and attend a school that offers public speaking classes. These are examples of actions, or the types of plans, you can take to yield you closer to your dreams.

So let's come up with a plan of action for you. The plan you choose will guide you so you will be able to accomplish your aspirations. As your partner I can help you think, envision, and role play. You need to feel comfortable enough to carry out your plan; otherwise all of your time and energy will be wasted.

Let's focus on your state of mind for a moment. At this point in your journey you may feel uncomfortable saying or doing things you are not accustomed to. It is to be expected that you may feel somewhat fearful, shy, or out of sorts. One way you may want to work through your uncomfortable moments may be by taking deep breaths and thinking of those who support you. Don't worry, I will give you support. I can be your sounding board and assist you during your decision-making process. Remember, you are on a mission to achieve your dreams. This can be a fantastic time for you.

So now I have several questions for you. You know what you want to accomplish. Now what are you willing to do to accomplish it? Do you need to take on more responsibilities or fewer responsibilities? Do you need to prevent someone from taking control over your life? Do you need to be calmer or have more pizzazz? Do you need to think about other people's feelings when you say or do something? I know I am asking you plenty of questions; and more questions are on the way. Why? Because this is how we begin to create the plan. This is when you decide how you will interact with others. In order to become successful in meeting your goals you must be mindful of yourself and others. For a brief moment you may want to look back at the goals you wrote down in Secret #4.

I feel one of the best parts about generating a plan is that you are preparing to take action. You are beginning to step out of your comfort zone and know it is time to tackle at least one of your life's problems or journey into a new territory. You can pat yourself on the back for having the courage to do this. You will be in awe when your plan is underway and you can see yourself clearly accomplishing your dreams.

For instance, you may want to be able to express your love or want to propose marriage to that special person. How can you get yourself to say this? Well, can you think of a location and time? Think about how you truly feel when you are with this person. Does your loved one take your breath away; make you feel a special way? Make you wonder when you will see him or her again? Thinking these types of thoughts can make it easier to go ahead with your plan.

Well, as your partner I can role play with you about what you would like to say. How do you think you would feel after you have proclaimed your love or proposed marriage? On the other hand, how do you feel now as a person who has not let your loved one know your true feelings? What is holding you back from taking the next step in your relationship? Do you truly love this person? Have you ever witnessed any friends or family members show affection towards each other? In the past, have you expressed love to someone or proposed marriage? Maybe some of these questions can spark ideas that can be helpful in generating a plan for a more meaningful relationship. If you desire to have a richer relationship with your partner, you can read "*Applying the Seven Secrets to Relationships*" in Part 2 of this book and use the relationship worksheets and charts for more intense guidance.

Another aspiration you may be seeking could be based on career mobility or acknowledgment in the workplace. When you are ready to have upward mobility at a company there are a few things you must find out. Of course it is highly suggested that you know how to articulate your thoughts and ideas and display work that will benefit the business. It is wise to do some homework, such as gathering information about the following: your boss, co-workers, the budget, and the best time to share your written and verbal ideas. You need to know what is required of you and the timeline for accomplishing tasks assigned to you. Also, I strongly suggest that your tasks should be completed prior to the deadline. Partner, you may want to consider some of these factors when you generate your career plan.

Let's be real; there are times when you feel you did everything perfectly. You and others may know you are the best candidate for a grand position. Yet someone else receives the position you yearned for. Now you have a few choices; one is to remain at the job and wait for another opportunity; you can choose to seek employment elsewhere; or you can even consider starting your own business.

Regardless of whatever you choose, you must continue to do your best. No slacking off. You never know who is watching you and when an opportunity will come your way. How do I know? People, including myself, have been offered leadership positions that we did not apply for while doing our best. So you never know. In addition, you will have gained some awesome skills while remaining at your present job.

Please do not forget to reveal your passion. Revealing your passion often gets you recognized and will get you to your end zone faster. As your partner, I can work with you to make sure these areas, as well as others, are covered. You may want to imagine yourself when you present your idea to your boss. Envision your boss's response. Visualize your co-worker's responses. You can create a script and you can also role play with me, your partner. Also consider role-playing with a friend or maybe a co-worker you trust. Think about how much time and energy you want to put into this idea that you want to present to your boss. Have you seen co-workers approach your boss? What type of respect does the boss show them? Have you observed their productivity, and how the boss views their work? Observe how passionate your co-workers are about their work.

While you are on your path to success, I recommend that you should have a neat appearance. If you are seeking a soul mate, a higher ranking position at your job, or just want to feel good about yourself, try to maintain your best look.

Now I will share a story about a man who knows the importance of generating a plan to look his best. Can you identify with this man? He is eager and determined to lose weight and has tried a few nutritional solutions. His goal is to be healthy and lose weight. He wants to lose at least seventy-five pounds. But for now his target is to lose thirty pounds within four months. He consulted with a doctor and found out he is allergic to nuts.

During the initial stage of his plan he hired fitness coaches so he could stay focused on exercising. Although that was an impressive move on his part, it did not solve his weight loss situation. The coaches were encouraging him to do strenuous exercises. This led him to wear body braces. When I asked him about his liquid and water intake he explained he does not drink nor like the taste of water, and he prefers to drink soft drinks. Then the next question was what type of foods does he eat? He stated that he usually eats junk foods because he does not cook. Can you identify with him now that you know a little more about him?

He has generated a new plan of action which consists of a three-part plan: exercise, liquid intake and food intake. His first decision is to continue with his personal trainers. Even though he feels the trainers push him too hard, he feels he needs to continue with the trainers because they help him to stay motivated. Also, when he is working out he remains focused on his vision of himself as a slimmer man. Therefore he continues exercising.

Now let's look at his new plan of action in regards to liquid intake. The plan was tailored towards his needs. This is when I stepped in as a life coach. These are some of the solutions we came up with: if he wanted to continue drinking soda there was a way in which he could do it without rapidly giving up soda. It was suggested that he buy a twelve-ounce bottle of soda and only drink four ounces with his meal. The slightest taste of soda would be all he needs to satisfy his palate. There is truly no need for him to drink a twelve-ounce bottle after each meal and snack. Besides, it is not healthy to drink a soda after each meal. We talked about the importance of drinking plenty of water. Remarkably, he quickly stopped drinking soda; and now drinks plenty of water.

In addition, we spoke about him trying to eat healthier foods - his third plan. He decided that when he is dining out, he will try to eat healthier meals. While eating fruit and raw nuts may have been a good suggestion, we know nuts are not for him. So he decided to eat grapes and apples as a snack food, and eat more fish and healthier foods as often as possible.

Presently he has lost twenty-five pounds. He drinks water and now enjoys the taste. He says he feels lighter, healthier and happier because his clothing size is smaller. Imagine when he loses his first fifty pounds — he will surely want to celebrate! However I suggested that he should not eat too much during his celebration.

This man found people to help him stick to his plan: his fitness coaches and fiance help him, and as his life coach, I also check up on his progress. So far his plan is successful and he is reaping the benefits of better health and a slimmer appearance. He still has a ways to go to achieve optimum health, but without a doubt, he is on his way. So, deciding on your plan then staying on the course of action are vital factors in accomplishing your dreams. Go to www.transformationplus.com to obtain 6 tips for a healthier life style.

A GUIDE TO FILLING OUT WORKSHEETS BASED ON A SPECIFIC VISION

In Secret # 3, there was a guide to help you fill out the *"My Vision"* worksheet based on a man's specific vision. Also, in Secret # 4 you filled out a "My Goals" worksheet. I will continue to give you a sample of how to decide on your plans based on a specific vision. Remember I am guiding you through a process. If you are considering owning a business you may differ in your approach. That's okay. My objective is to walk you through a process from a vision to action planning. The following is a reminder of a man's vision and goals to own his own bakery.

Secret # 3: My Vision

I see myself at a bakery store, wearing a baker's hat and white apron. I see other people working along side of me in my small shop wearing their aprons and hats with smiles on their faces. Yes, this is my shop. I can smell the sweet aroma of cakes, pies and cookies. I see the flour, dough and fruits such as strawberries and blueberries. I just finished preparing a cake and I am now presenting it to a customer. My customers are happy and have a smile on their face when they pick up their pastry we made for their special occasions. I am especially happy when my customers come back to my store and say they truly enjoyed the pastries we baked. My small shop is located in my neighborhood. Many of my customers know me.

Secret # 4: My Goal

My goal is to own a bakery shop. Why? I have dreamed often about it. When I bake pastries many people have complimented me and even asked me if I considered starting my own business. I have saved the money so this is a good time.

Now let's look at the plans based on a man's vision.

Secret # 5: My Plans
Do: Find a location to open the shop
Do: Interview and hire staff
Do: Obtain and process legal documents needed to own business and speak with lawyer(s)

Let's use your goals to guide you so that you can create your plans. When you decide each plan, can you imagine yourself doing and saying what you set out to accomplish? If you can imagine it, you are on your way to creating a great plan. Now I want you to take some time to come up with possible plans that can help you reach your goals.

Use the *"My Plans"* worksheet page that follows to record your thoughts and write your plans based on what you want to say and/or do. When filling out your plan for action please consider adding as many details as possible. The more information you write the easier it could be to follow through.

My Plans

① Say:

   Do:

② Say:

   Do:

③ Say:

   Do:

④ Say:

   Do:

⑤ Say:

   Do:

Secret # 5: How to Generate a Plan

SELF-DISCOVERY CHECKPOINT:

It is time for another self-discovery check. Let's find out how you are feeling right now since you just finished writing your plans. We want you to become more successful in your personal and professional life, so answer these questions very truthfully.

STRESS LEVEL ASSESSMENT

1. **What is your present stress level from 1 through 10? Please circle your response.**

(1 = very low stress level, 5 = some stress, 10 = very high stress level).

Stress Number Line

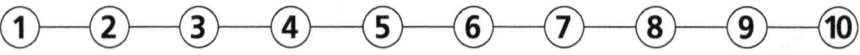

2. **What stresses are you experiencing right now, if any? Explain.**

3. **Based on the Stress vs. Success balance beams that follow:**
   i. Which of the 3 diagrams best represents you?
      a. Stress is overpowering (you feel unable to handle your stress)
      b. I can succeed/ Success is possible (you can control it and feel more success than stress)
      c. Balanced (you feel some stress, but hope is in sight)

   ii. Which diagram best describes how you feel when you are involved with others on a personal or professional basis?
      a. Stress is overpowering
      b. I can succeed/ Success is possible
      c. Balanced

Stress vs. Success

Stress is over powering (a)   or   I can succeed/ Success is possible (b)

Balanced (c)

Secret # 5: How to Generate a Plan

4. **Do you feel you can achieve success in the near future?**
   Yes ___ No ___

   i. If yes, in what ways do you feel you can be successful?

   ii. If no, why not?

5. **How would you rank your energy level on a scale of 1 through 10? Please circle your response.**

   (1= very low, 5= some energy, 10= very high)

   Energy Level Number Line

   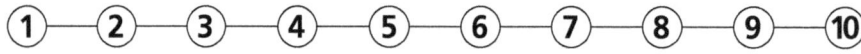

Secret # 6:
Discover How to Timeline Your Tasks

Congratulations! You have generated a plan. Now we need to set a time frame. *"Timeline Your Tasks"* is the key to unlocking your sixth Secret to achieve your dreams. It is not suggested that you go to work tomorrow and show your proposal to your boss after reading this book. Maybe you will be successful without any thought of planning. If you succeed, that is great! But if you crash, we would have to pick up all the pieces. Or the worst could happen; you may not want to fulfill that objective anymore because the results were not what you wanted. You may become discouraged, ashamed or angry. So why take the chance when the odds would be highly in your favor after you have practiced and done your homework? You need to feel confident and know you are ready to meet the challenges you are about to face. A time schedule would most likely be the best bet.

So let's take a few moments to create a timeline. Do you want to accomplish your tasks in three months? Maybe it will take three months to build up the courage, through role playing, to express your love to your partner. If you want to develop a stronger relationship with a loved one, yet you are spending most of your time with friends, your three-month plan of action may be to spend more time with your loved one. This will give your partner time to see how serious you are about the relationship.

I want to speak briefly about matters concerning career advancement. It may take six months or even a year based on how you are presently rated at your job and the type of reputation you have thus far, to achieve an objective. Timelines may also require some prerequisites that may need to be added to the plan as we go along. Is your attendance at the job poor and do you arrive late to work? These factors will most likely hinder you from getting that ideal career position immediately, even if you have the necessary qualifications. As a result you may want to work on eliminating hindrances first. Keep in mind it could take months before the boss notices your change.

I have a few more questions. Do you think this is the appropriate time to pursue your dreams? Would the person you want to impress, whether a boss or loved one, be available? Why do you feel you should get a new position or change your relationship status now? When would you like to begin to pursue your plans and when would you like to achieve them? How much time do you want to invest in each task? And are you going to give it your all immediately or move at a slow pace?

In Secret #5 "How to Generate a Plan" we probed into how you plan to reach your goals, and what your approach will be. Also in the same secret, you wrote what you plan to do or say to achieve your dreams. Therefore you may want to use the "*My Plans*" worksheet you filled out in Secret # 5 as your guide. Since we are now in the timeline section, the focus is on creating a time frame in which you will do each of the things you wrote about in the "*My Plans*" section. I am going to refer to the plans you want to accomplish as your principal task and mini tasks. By no means should the mini tasks be taken for granted. Each mini task requires plenty of action on your part.

Now you have to keep in mind, some principal tasks can take more than a year to accomplish. This is why mini tasks are needed. Mini tasks can help you stay focused on your ultimate objective. In addition you will feel content because you have achieved some results in a shorter period of time. You may want to consider at least three mini tasks for each principal task you want to achieve. Also add next to each one a date or time frame when you think you could accomplish each of the tasks.

For example, your principal task may be to lose seventy pounds in 12 months. Three mini tasks can be the following:

a) Look for and consult with a nutritionist, learn about healthier, satisfying foods and begin eating them within two months.

b) Have plenty of water available for you to drink and carry water with you often. Start within one month.

c) Increase your exercise to four times per week: go to gym, work out with friends and/or set up exercise space at home. Begin within three to five months,

Partner, this part of your journey involves action which is planned out. Along the way some of your ideas may have to be altered or maybe new ones may have to be added. Regardless, the timeline gives us structure as to how we can approach your plans and certainly when you want to take that leap towards success.

I gave you a weight reduction plan for the timeline. However we must take up again the baker's vision so that I can continue to guide you through the process of achieving your dreams. So far we learned about a man's vision, goals and plans. Next we are going to put his plans into a timeline. But let's review everything the man wrote.

A GUIDE TO FILLING OUT WORKSHEETS BASED ON A SPECIFIC VISION

Secret # 3: My Vision

I see myself at a bakery store, wearing a baker's hat and white apron. I see other people working along side of me in my small shop wearing their aprons and hats with smiles on their faces. Yes, this is my shop. I can smell the sweet aroma of cakes, pies and cookies. I see the flour, dough and fruits such as strawberries and blueberries. I just finished preparing a cake and I am now presenting it to a customer. My customers are happy and have a smile on their face when they pick up their pastry we made for their special occasions. I am especially happy when my customers come back to my store and say they truly enjoyed the pastries we baked. My small shop is located in my neighborhood. Many of my customers know me.

Secret # 4: My Goals

My goal is to own a bakery shop. Why? I have dreamed often about it. When I bake pastries many people have complimented me and even asked me if I considered starting my own business. I have saved the money so this is a good time to start my own business.

Secret # 5: My Plans

Do: Research bakery business
Do: Research owning a store
Do: Find a location to open the shop
Do: Interview and hire staff
Do: Obtain and process legal documents needed to own business and speak with lawyer(s)

Now let's look at the timeline based on this man's vision.

Secret # 6: Timeline

1. Principal Task
Own and operate a bakery. Date to be accomplished: **9 months***

a. Mini Task
Research bakery business. Date to be accomplished: **2 months**

b. Mini Task
Research owning a store. Date to be accomplished: **3 months**

c. Mini Task
Find a location for the shop. Date to be accomplished: **6 months**

d. Mini Task
Obtain legal documents. Date to be accomplished: **7 months**

e. Mini Task
Interview and hire 3 staff members
Date to be accomplished: **8 months**

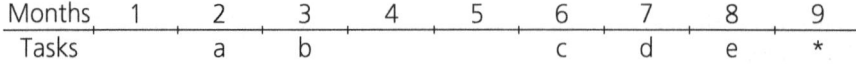

Months	1	2	3	4	5	6	7	8	9
Tasks		a	b			c	d	e	*

Part 1. Revealing the Seven Secrets to Achieve Your Dreams

On the "*Timeline*" worksheet write what you plan to do as well as when you plan to achieve it. Then place the information on the timeline.

Timeline

(1) Principal Task: ....

Date to be accomplished:

(a) Mini Task: ....

Date to be accomplished:

(b) Mini Task: ....

Date to be accomplished:

(c) Mini Task: ....

Date to be accomplished:

(d) Mini Task: ....

Date to be accomplished:


```
Months   1   2   3   4   5   6   7   8   9
Tasks
```

Secret # 6: Discover How to Timeline Your Tasks

Partner, begin doing all of the tasks you wrote on your timeline. Start accomplishing your mini tasks. While you are accomplishing your objectives you can check them off and feel great about yourself. When you receive positive feedback from friends, family and co-workers then you will feel even better. These mini tasks will give you the boost needed to hang in there while you are striving towards your principal task- your dream.

If you feel you need to add more tasks, do so. However do not forget to add when you plan to accomplish that objective. When all of the mini tasks are achieved, you should feel ready to accomplish your final objective. This is when you can look in the mirror and practice what you want to say to your boss or loved one at least a day or two prior to the big day; or you can practice how you will greet your customers on opening day tomorrow at your bakery, or you can look at yourself in the mirror and say to yourself, "Wow! I lost plenty of weight. I look and feel great." Isn't this exciting?

For the man who wants to own his own bakery- he should have done his research, found his shop, taken care of his legal documents, and hired his employees.

Secret # 7: You Have Arrived! Now Live Your Dreams!

This is great! You have the key to unlock Secret # 7 *"Live Your Dreams!"* Now you will be able to do just that. Achieve your dreams!

Since you have accomplished your objectives, and have demonstrated how responsible, motivated and sincere you are, you should feel comfortable and confident enough to make your grand dream become a reality. If you need to, practice your script one more time while looking in a mirror. That is fine.

Today you may want to go up to your partner and express your affection, or present your dynamic proposal for upward mobility to your boss or do whatever you set out to accomplish. As for the man who had a vision of becoming a proprietor, he now has the key to open his own bakery. It is time to do it, say it, show it, sing it, or shout it. Live your dreams.

How do you feel? Guess what? Regardless of the outcome, you did your part and you will be rewarded one way or another. I have experienced this, as have so many others who have strived for one thing and received something bigger, better and greater.

Congratulations on your progress this far. You thought about it, envisioned it, planned it, and executed it. Now it is time to reap the benefits. In reality you have already reaped benefits by accomplishing your mini tasks. You can pat yourself on the back for a job well done. Be ready to make more progress. The next two parts of the book focus exclusively on relationships and careers, respectively. As you read and do the exercises to enhance your relationship and career you will acquire more opportunities for success.

Remember the "*My Strengths*" worksheet page, which was part of the first chapter? Well now you can add more 'strengths' to your profile, such as, you are a motivated person — one who can accomplish goals. Also, you can now go to the "*Life's Problems*" page and cross out that challenge you just overcame.

When you have time please reflect on the process you used to help you to accomplish your dreams, on the "*You Did It!*" and "*Self-discovery Checkpoint*" worksheet pages that follow. Think about the beginning when you were pondering on your life's problems, up to and including your positive end results. The reflection will assist you when you are ready to take on your next challenge. In the meantime, revel in your success. Once again, congratulations!

Reading to obtain knowledge is great. Achieving your dreams - PRICELESS!

You Did It!

1. What did you accomplish?

2. What did you learn about yourself?

3. How do you feel?

Secret # 7: You Have Arrived! Now Live Your Dreams!

SELF-DISCOVERY CHECKPOINT:

It is time for another self-discovery check. Let's find out how you are feeling right now since you just finished writing your plans. We want you to become more successful in your personal and professional life, so answer these questions very truthfully.

STRESS LEVEL ASSESSMENT

1. **What is your present stress level from 1 through 10? Please circle your response.**

(1 = very low stress level, 5 = some stress, 10 = very high stress level).

Stress Number Line

2. **What stresses are you experiencing right now, if any? Explain.**

3. **Based on the Stress vs. Success balance beams that follow:**

    i. Which of the 3 diagrams best represents you?

       a. Stress is overpowering (you feel unable to handle your stress)

       b. I can succeed/ Success is possible (you can control it and feel more success than stress)

       c. Balanced (you feel some stress, but hope is in sight)

    ii. Which diagram best describes how you feel when you are involved with others on a personal or professional basis?

       a. Stress is overpowering

       b. I can succeed/ Success is possible

       c. Balanced

Stress vs. Success

Stress — Success Joy
or
Success Joy — Stress

Stress is over powering (a)

I can succeed/ Success is possible (b)

Balanced (c)

Secret # 7: You Have Arrived! Now Live Your Dreams!

4. **Do you feel you can achieve success in the near future?**
   Yes ___ No ___

   i. If yes, in what ways do you feel you can be successful?

   ii. If no, why not?

5. **How would you rank your energy level on a scale of 1 through 10? Please circle your response.**

   (1= very low, 5= some energy, 10= very high)

   Energy Level Number Line

   Your self discovery check results should be great, especially because you completed your tasks and had success learning new and wonderful things about yourself. Do you feel awesome? Do you feel uplifted?

Part 2

How to Apply the Seven Secrets to Relationships

"Love is not about finding the right person, but creating a right relationship. It's not about how much love you have in the beginning but how much love you build till the end."

Anonymous

Relationships

We all know it is so easy to get caught up in the day-to-day rut of repeating and doing the same things over and over again. Aspirations and dreams are slowly put on the back burner or may vanish from our minds because we are caught up in daily routines. Enjoying nature and people can become less of a priority. People get involved in performing tasks as opposed to showing affection and caring for others. When was the last time you told someone special you loved them? When was the last time you tried to create more harmony in your relationship with someone special - a friend, family member or loved one?

This section of the book is devoted to action-takers who are interested in building their relationship with someone. I will guide you as to how you can apply the *"Seven Secrets to Achieve Your Dreams"* design for the relationship you desire. For optimum results, it is suggested that you read Part 1 of this book, *"Revealing the Seven Secrets"* first. As your coach and partner I can guide you; however, I am not a psychologist, counselor nor any type of specialist. Please contact a specialist for more intense interventions. As always, it is up to you to decide the path you wish to take.

Let's help you grow richer in your relationships. Isn't that what you want? Great! Each secret will focus exclusively on relationships. I want to help you strengthen your relationships with family members, friends and loved ones. Therefore the questions you will be asked will be for the purpose of helping you to discover your pathway to success. Your journey will require you to focus on what you can do. My objective is to help you to transform your life into something more wonderful than it is at the present time. You may want more commitment in the relationship, or your relationship may be falling apart. Either way, I can give you some guidance, especially if guidance is what you are seeking.

As your partner, I can help you think, envision and do some role-playing. Remember you are not alone. I want you to feel comfortable knowing you have me as a supporter during this challenging time in your life. You will be asked to record information on worksheets and exercises just as you did on the first part of the book. Are you ready to begin your journey? Fantastic!

Secret# 1: How to Identify Your Strengths

Remember when we were uncovering the Seven Secrets to Achieve Your Dreams? You were asked to write about your strengths in Secret #1. Now we are going to focus exclusively on your relationship with a specific person. I have a few questions I would like you to answer. What are some of the positive attributes you possess in this relationship? Do you cook great meals for your partner? Do you plan several activities for both of you to enjoy? Are you a provider? I will end with this question: Do you pay attention to your partner? Well, if you possess all of these strengths I hope your significant other, friend or family member has complimented you about these great qualities at some point in your relationship. If your partner has not, I will. You are doing a great job.

I will use the terms "significant other" or "your partner" to define the person you want to build your relationship with throughout this part of the book.

I just want to let you know that having strengths are the key to your success. So continue to do the great things you are doing. I want to add something; do not feel embarrassed when you do nice things to make your relationship a richer one with your partner. Keep your self confidence positive. Continue to focus on what you can do. Make great things happen in both of your lives.

I would like you to focus your attention on the "My Strengths" worksheet. Unlike the other "My Strengths' charts in Part 1 of this book, you are going to focus exclusively on your adult years. Write in the section provided "Things I Enjoy Doing with My Partner." An example of this could be that you enjoy jogging with your partner. Next, jot down in the appropriate section "Things I Like to Do for My Partner." Maybe you like to bake desserts. Last, but not least, write characteristics that make you special such as you are an excellent listener, in the "What Makes Me So Special" section. Enjoy reminiscing and writing about these positive qualities you bring to the relationship. I suggest that you revisit this section of the book, or the first "My Strengths" worksheet page, especially if you need a positive boost. So do not leave out any of your great characteristics.

My Strengths

Things I Enjoy Doing with My Partner

1.

2.

3.

Things I Like to Do for My Partner

1.

2.

3

What Makes Me So Special?

1.

2.

3.

Part 2. How to Apply the Seven Secrets to Relationships

Secret #2:
How to Survey Your Life's Problems

Let's survey your life's problems. If you wrote anything about your relationship with a friend, family member or a romantic partnership as one of your life's problems in Part 1 of this book, I know you are probably ready to take on this challenge. If you did not include any type of relationship as one of your life's problems, think about it for a moment. Is this an area you want to probe into right now? If not, this section may not be for you. However, you are more than welcomed to gain some insight, share it with others or use the information if your relationship with a loved one becomes an issue in the future. Or maybe *"How to Apply the Seven Secrets to Career Advancement"* or the bonus section, *"Especially for Older Adults"* would be a better section for you to explore.

Now we are going to explore deeper into your life's problems. Do you have difficulty expressing your true feelings? Do you feel you are not good enough to be with this person? Are you being taken for granted? Do you feel your partner is taking advantage of you? Do you always rely on your partner or vice versa? By the time you get home from work, are you exhausted and not willing to interact with your loved one? Are you unsure of yourself and your role in the relationship?

Do you want to tell your partner you want a more involved relationship? If your answer is yes, then what is holding you back? For example, are you shy? Do you feel you are not courageous? Do you have a fear of commitment? Do you have a fear that the person you love does not want to be in a committed relationship with you? Do you feel you have a communication problem? Do you feel there is a generation gap that separates the two of you? Are you reflecting on past experiences? Do you love this person? How do you presently feel by not proclaiming your true feelings? Partner, if you feel you have some difficulty expressing your feelings, and you are displeased with the present stage of your relationship, we have some work ahead of us.

Women, who want a romantic relationship, keep in mind that men are characterized as hunters. I have read books and attended several workshops hosted by men both young and mature in age, stating the same information I am providing in this paragraph. Since a man is a hunter, you can accept his advances, but you can not be the initiator; at least in the earlier stages of your relationship. If he does not initiate dating, dining, communicating, etc., then you have choices. Either you can wait for his advances and/or date other men. Trying to get a man to love you by giving him gifts, etc. and catering to his personal desires will not create a richer relationship between you and 'your' man. So what I am saying is — allow him to say and prove he loves you first. This will mean the world of difference in your quest for a fulfilling relationship.

Are you ready to learn more about your relationship and how to make the relationship a richer one? If you are ready to continue the journey, then let's start by taking a few deep breaths. Inhale, exhale, and once again inhale, now exhale. Great!

I feel we need to speak about the relationship you have with your partner in general. How long have you been in a relationship with this person? What do you admire about each other? There must be something holding you together. Some type of chemistry. Define it! This next question isn't as pleasant: what are the pitfalls and baggage each of you brings to the relationship? One important thing we must also consider is how you handle yourself when your partner does not cooperate or agree with you. For example, do you find yourself withdrawing or do you become aggressive when things do not go your way?

Think about how you communicate and what both of you are spending your time communicating about. Do you share your emotions and feelings with each other? How often and at what level? What is the level of commitment? Where would you like to see this relationship heading in the future? Do you know how your partner will respond to the previous question? Is this a relationship where you give each other plenty of space, some free time away from each other; or do both parties do everything together? How do both of you feel about that? Are you both giving your all to make this relationship work, or is one person doing most of the work? And my final question is, do you trust each other?

This next section is for married couples. Are you married with children? We know there are times during a marriage when couples experience ups and downs. Is your marriage experience unpleasant? Is there a feeling in your gut that something is not right, but you are unable to pinpoint it or do not have proof to substantiate your feeling?

Have you had the following type of experience? Let's start by saying neither of you want to receive marriage counseling. However, both of you agree to go on a family vacation in another state, even though there is much turmoil in your marriage. Wouldn't this seem like a great idea, the whole family vacationing together?

Unfortunately both of you continue to argue and fight during the trip. This creates an unhappy environment for everyone. One of you disappears and decides to go back home, leaving the other parent with the children. I am sure you would not want to continue vacationing under these circumstances. You are concerned about the safety of your spouse, the one who has left. Nonetheless you become angry because your spouse left you and the children. If you were the one who left, you must have a burning need to leave your spouse and children. Have you had a similar experience? Did your similar experience eventually lead to a divorce?

This type of situation adds more stress and tension to a marriage. My point is that I do not suggest that you travel together and use a vacation as a means of making the relationship richer. Solve your problems first; then think about traveling and celebrating later. Partner, you may decide to take the chance and travel with your spouse while experiencing hardship. If everything works out, that's fantastic! However, if arguing and fighting occurs, it may be hard to pick up the pieces. Do you really want to take the chance of breaking up your marriage?

Although I stated the previous section was for married couples, the same suggestion applies for those going on a vacation with a friend or family member. If you and this person are at wit's end with each other, you may want to avoid traveling together during that time of turmoil.

I want to share with you what I have heard several psychologists say concerning one general difference between men and women. Remember the word 'general' means that it does not apply in every case, but applies in most cases. Women generally spend more time thinking about something that bothers them, more than men do. However, a man leaves the negative thought behind by the end of the day. So if you are a woman who is trying to make the relationship richer, keep in mind that it may take you a little longer to let go of your emotional discontent. If you are a male trying to develop this relationship and you are ready to move on because the issue is finished as far as you are concerned, you should be aware that she may not be ready when you are. However, it is important that you be sensitive towards her for a little while longer; at least until she moves out of her emotional zone.

Let's probe a little deeper in terms of what is going on at home. This applies to those who live in the same household. Is one person doing all of the household chores and working full time? Does this describe your partner? Or are you the one working and doing all the household chores? Well, if your partner is the one doing all the household chores and has a full time job, I strongly suggest that you should help. Are you trying to build a richer relationship? Helping your partner is one way you surely can.

I have a few suggestions. I will begin with suggestions based on you, if you are the one who is not offering to give a helping hand. Start by observing the body language and attitude of your loved one while you are relaxing and not offering a helping hand. Does your partner seem content watching you while you are relaxing around the house? When your partner completes the chores do you have a sufficient amount of quality time with him/her? Or does your partner seem exhausted? I wonder what the response would be if you asked your partner how he/she feels about doing so much. Have you offered to help and your partner refused your assistance? If yes, why did your partner refuse your help? Please watch your partner carefully; your loved one may not be complaining aloud to you. We know complaining aloud or displaying an attitude of discontent will not bring forth a good relationship nor maintain a good marriage. Maybe your partner does not want to be perceived as a nagger.

Why don't you have a conversation and offer to help by choosing to do a chore or two to alleviate the stress so you can bring some harmony into the relationship? Your partner will appreciate you. Isn't this what you want — to be appreciated?

Now let's flip the script. Are you the one doing all of the household tasks and working? Why? Do not take for granted that your loved one already knows how you feel. Therefore, you may want to express your feelings to your partner. However — do not nag. If you do all of the chores, you have probably spoken with your loved one already. It is important to observe your partner to see if there is a hidden agenda to keep you busy and tired while your partner is relaxed and able to participate in activities that do not include you. Or are you doing this to avoid some type of interaction with your loved one? If either is the case, then your relationship needs some major work.

On a more positive note, you may ask your partner to do a single chore. Let your loved one choose his or her preferred chore. If your partner refuses, you can continue to do everything as in the past, hire a maid or dissolve the relationship. I do not suggest dissolving the relationship because your spouse did not want to help out. However, be conscious of your quality time together and what you get in return for all of your hard work and consistent efforts.

If you plan to see a marriage counselor, I suggest you do not confide in someone you or your partner knows. This person already has their own opinion about both of you and this may cause a conflict of interest. Even if the counselor has the best of intentions, at some point one of you may feel your interest is not being served. You may consider having a friend counsel you because this person may do it for free or at an inexpensive price. Do you really want your counselor friend to know all of your personal, intimate business?

I think this is a good time to mention sex. Yes, sex. Sexual intercourse plays an important part in a couple's relationship. Are both of you truthfully sharing your emotions and feeling satisfied before, during and after intercourse? And what does 'satisfied' mean to each of you? You may want to spend some time thinking and answering these questions and others, such as how past relationships have impacted on you at the present time. Both of you should feel free of insecurities about your past experiences.

If the only thing you both do when you are together is have sex, you have a few choices. One option is to look forward to meeting your partner for purposes of having sex. But keep in mind this may be the only thing keeping the relationship together. Concerning this type of relationship, I want to ask you a few questions. How would you rate yourself on the following two questions, on a scale from 1 through 3? (1= unhappy, 2= do not care, 3= happy). Please be very truthful to yourself. How do you feel when your partner leaves you after having sex? How do you feel when you see other couples in public enjoying each others' company? This second question is for you if you do not go out as a couple. If you scored a one on either of these questions, you have options. One option is to have a conversation about your feelings. After a short period of time if there are no changes in your relationship, you may want to consider another option.

Maybe you will want to choose to end the relationship and move on to someone who will enjoy your company, respect you, pay attention to you and be sensitive to your needs. It may seem like I am addressing only women. However, I know men who are having similar types of experiences.

Since you want this relationship to grow richer you probably do not want to waste time with someone who does not see you as part of their future. Once again you need to have conversations about your future together.

Through your conversations you can learn more about your friend, family member or romantic partner. Watch the body language and the eyes. Is this person making eye contact with you? Does this person look like he/she is taking you for granted? Please keep in mind their actions will tell you everything you need to know. So observe. Now, if your partner prefers not to communicate, that may be a telling sign that things may not be in your favor. However it could be about his/her personal "stuff" that he/she does not want to share with you.

I do not have to remind you that this is your loving partner. I know I often say I am your partner, however, you and I both know I am your supporter. I want to help you make a healthy transition in your personal life. I want you to grow richer in your personal life by developing your relationship with your significant other. So think about the questions I asked you. Look at the *"Life's Problems"* worksheet page that follows. Now write the type of challenges you are facing in this relationship. The focus is on your life's problems as an adult. It can be problems you face with a friend, a family member or your romantic partner.

Life's Problems

1.

2.

3.

4.

Since we are still surveying your life's problems, let's move to another level. Do you have concerns? Has your loved one told you he or she loves you or likes you? If your partner has said it to you that's great! However I sense something must be going on as to why you have not reciprocated your feelings, or seem to need help trying to move the relationship to another level. I need to ask you a few questions concerning this. Why have you not expressed nor shown your partner how you feel? How do you react when your partner expresses his/her feelings? Do you feel your partner is sincere? Does your partner want you around so that you can pay their way, or be their chauffeur? Do you feel your partner has an ulterior motive? I mean, do you feel your partner expresses his/her feelings just to get something from you? Does your loved one say I love you too frequently or in such a way that it does not seem to impress you? Then how would you best be impressed? How often is too frequent? Have you spoken with your partner about it?

I know you love/like your partner - that's why you are still reading this section of the book. I hope you are ready for my next set of questions. When your partner says he/she loves you, which of the following approaches, if any, bothers you the most? When your partner says "I love you", where is it said, how is it said, or why is it said? For instance is it always said over the telephone or a text message, even though both of you see each other often? Or is it said to obtain something of value such as money, citizenship or intimacy?

Still on the topic of concerns, does your partner ask you for much but rarely gives? Is your partner available often, when you need him/her, or rarely? Do you feel you are not allowed in their physical or emotional space?

For people who were married in the past I have several questions for you. Are you concerned that you want to get married but your partner has stated he/she only wants companionship? Are you willing to remain in the relationship, with your partner, under these circumstances, because you do not want to live alone? Do you fear being alone?

If each of you were married in the past and have your own home do you have concerns about living arrangements? Do you have concerns which could involve prenuptial agreements? Does one or both of you have young children or adult children who live with you and the presence of the child is causing a conflict? Do you have a family member who insists your loved one is not good for you? Do you feel there is something in the way of your progress? And my final question is: do you believe there is someone else your partner may be interested in other than you? You need to explore your thoughts and any fears you may have. Write these concerns on the "*My Concerns*" worksheet.

My Concerns

1.

2.

3.

4.

Part 2. How to Apply the Seven Secrets to Relationships

You may want to take a power break. Let's take a few deep breaths. Inhale, now exhale. Once again inhale and exhale. Maybe you want to stand up and walk around for a few minutes as well as have a sip of tea or water. Are you ready to continue? Great!

If your partner has expressed their love to you, has written it to you, and/or spends plenty of quality time with you, yet you do not feel at ease enough to express it in return, then it could be based on your own experiences and views or it could be some suspicion you have about your partner. Either way, you know how you feel and at some point you want to feel comfortable enough to express your love. Your choices range from holding off expressing your love until another day, having a conversation about your relationship, or giving in to your true feelings and observing your partner's actions and reactions. Do you want to stay at this present state of mind - thinking and wondering? Let's do a self-discovery check to find out how you are feeling and your current state of energy.

SELF-DISCOVERY CHECKPOINT:

Remember we want you to become more successful in your personal life. Also I want you to stay focused on your objectives, and help you monitor your progress. So answer these questions very truthfully. Please refer to the *"How to Evaluate the Self-discovery Check"* located in Part 1 of the book. After you acknowledge your stress level and energy level scores, you will know when it is best to proceed to the next chapter.

STRESS LEVEL ASSESSMENT

1. **What is your present stress level from 1 through 10? Please circle your response.**

(1 = very low stress level, 5 = some stress, 10 = very high stress level).

Stress Number Line

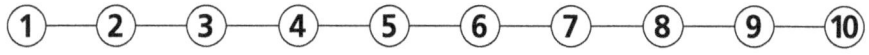

2. **What stresses are you experiencing right now, if any? Explain.**

3. Based on the Stress vs. Success balance beams that follow:

   i. Which of the 3 diagrams best represents you?

      a. Stress is overpowering

      b. I can succeed/ Success is possible

      c. Balanced

   ii. Which diagram best describes how you feel when you are with your partner?

      a. Stress is overpowering

      b. I can succeed/ Success is possible

      c. Balanced

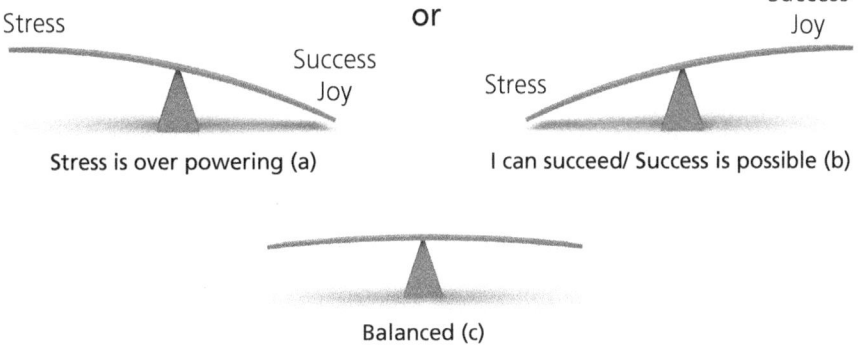

4. **Do you feel you can achieve success in your relationship? Yes ___ No ___**

   i. If yes, in what ways do you feel you can be successful?

   ii. If no, why not?

5. **How would you rank your energy level on a scale of 1 through 10? Please circle your response.**

   (1= very low, 5= some energy, 10= very high)

   Energy Level Number Line

   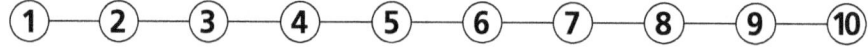

   Partner, these questions I have asked you are to help you to understand your relationship with your loved one, so that you can get in touch with your inner self; where you presently stand, and where you want to ultimately go. Remember, the key to your success is to think positively, positively, positively! Are you ready to move on? Fantastic!

Part 2. How to Apply the Seven Secrets to Relationships

Secret # 3:
Discover How to Envision Your Dreams

Using Secret #3 we are going to discover how to envision your dream — your dream to create a richer relationship between you and your loved one. Your visions are your dreams or thoughts of someone who you want to build your relationship with. Keep in mind that if you cannot imagine yourself saying and doing what you've envisioned when you are alone, then you may have difficulty saying and doing these things when your partner is in front of you. We want you to discover your limitations as well as allow you to understand how far your imagination can take you. In addition, I have created a *"My Vision"* worksheet in order to help you to acknowledge what you truly want and to assist you in ultimately accomplishing your visions.

I want you to look at the *"My Vision"* worksheet and have a pencil ready, along with two small pictures available - one of you and one of your loved one. Write your name and your partner's name. Place the two pictures at the middle of the page. Great!

My Vision

....

(Place partner's picture
and name above the line)

(Place your name
and picture above the line)

Take a deep breath — inhale and exhale. Once again inhale in, now exhale out. Very good! Now look at the picture of your partner and the one of yourself. I want you to bring the thoughts, dreams and visions you have in your mind to the surface. Now let's begin the envisioning process. I want you to imagine yourself in a more involved relationship with this special person. Begin to put a smile on your face while you are using your imagination, and think about your location. What are you doing together? What are each of you saying? What are the two of you wearing? Are you walking in the sand on a beach while the sun is setting? Are you dancing outdoors in the moonlight on a cruise ship? Does your vision involve traveling together, doing activities together, getting married, starting a family or having more children? Take it all in. Breathe it, feel it and say it all in your imagination. Have fun imagining. How do you feel? Remember, you want a richer relationship with your partner.

Let's go a step further into your imagination. Take those deep breaths again. Breathe in, breathe out. Breathe in and breathe out. Re-imagine your life with your loved one. Close your eyes while imagining these wonderful thoughts. When you are ready, open your eyes and jot down the thoughts you just envisioned.

Were your thoughts pleasant? Did your partner appear to accept your vision? While you were in your imaginative state of mind, did your partner appear pleased? If yes, that is great!

If you envisioned some discomfort between your partner and yourself, then we need to understand where this feeling is coming from so we can move you toward your comfort zone. A suggestion — change your imaginative setting, time of day or other factors until you feel comfortable with your imagined picture. Keep a positive outlook. When you feel content with your vision, then we can move on to the next secret.

Secret # 4: How to Create Your Goals

Let's begin to create goals for a richer relationship for you. I want to define goals as those things you want to accomplish. The things you are aiming for in your life - your hopes, your aspirations. For example if you envisioned yourself doing activities with your partner, you may want to make that a goal you want to achieve. We know you truly love this person; otherwise you would not be focusing so much energy and time on the relationship.

Answer these questions: Do you want to continue to put the time and energy into the relationship? Is your partner often, part-time or rarely available? For example, do you live together or is this person overseas fighting in a war? Do you feel it is important to act as soon as possible or take it somewhat slow?

On a scale from 1 to 5 (1= most casual, 5 = most serious), how would you rate the quality of your relationship? Is it a serious one or a causal one? On the number line that follows, circle the number which best describes your interpretation of the quality of the relationship. If possible, ask your partner what he/she feels the quality of the relationship is.

A. Quality of the relationship with your partner (your response)

B. Quality of the relationship (partner's response)

The more insight you receive from your partner, the better chance of developing a richer relationship. However, if you do not ask your partner you can guess what his or her response will be; but keep in mind that a guess is nothing more than a guess. As your coach and partner I may have to help you shape and reshape your goals. It's okay! I will guide you through your goal-reaching process.

Now what goals do you wish to achieve? What is your first goal, your second goal; and why are you choosing these goals? As you are thinking of a few goals? I want to ask you a few more questions. Are these realistic goals? Do you feel you will be able to reach the first goal in a timely manner? Do you feel we need to break through some uncomfortable barriers prior to working on the goal? Therefore, those barriers can become goals that need to be met, as well. You may want to consider choosing goals you feel you can accomplish quickly; as well as goals you feel are of utmost importance

Your focus is to write down goals based on your vision. Let me start by saying some goals, in this case, mini goals can lead you towards your principal vision. As you check off the goals that you've accomplished in a short period of time, you know you are getting closer to your grand vision, the big picture of what you want to ultimately accomplish with your loved one. This goal cannot, in most cases, be done overnight. I want you to know that while you continue to complete your mini goals/tasks you will become more content and your energy level will probably be high because you are making progress.

Part 2. How to Apply the Seven Secrets to Relationships

For now I would like you to jot down some goals. So I ask that you review the "My Vision" worksheet from Secret # 3 to give you some guidance as to the type of goals you would like to create. Now take some time to think and write down at least three goals — and why you are choosing these particular goals on the "My Goals" worksheet.

My Goals

1.

Why?

2.

Why?

3.

Why?

Part 2. How to Apply the Seven Secrets to Relationships

Secret # 5: How to Generate a Plan

It is time to "*Generate a Plan.*" You must decide on the approach you will use to make your goals become a reality. In other words - how you will go about having the relationship you want, and what your plan of action is. Let me state why it is important to generate a plan for the purpose of enhancing your relationship with your partner. Your plan will guide you so that you can accomplish your goals. You already know you are feeling some discomfort while trying to create a stronger relationship, otherwise we would not be spending time on this. However, we also know you are interested in advancing the relationship to a more serious level.

So let's take a power break. You may want to stand up, stretch out and take some deep breaths. Let's inhale, exhale. Once again inhale, now exhale. At this time you may also want to take in the aromatic smell of the candle if you have one nearby, and drink some relaxing herbal tea or water. Are you ready to continue the journey? Are you ready to write your plan of action? Great!

Now I would like you to measure your level of seriousness based on the next question. On a number value from 1 through 5, how serious are you about achieving your vision? Circle your response.

1 = not serious

2 = somewhat serious

3 = casual

4 = serious

5 = very serious

Now that you have chosen your answer please refer back to your "quality of the relationship" response you wrote in Secret #4. Are the responses similar? If you did not circle serious or very serious, please stop and rethink what you really want. We are about half way through your self-discovery journey. You must remember this: one of my goals as your coach is to keep you focused. However, the ultimate answers come from within. You will be able to find solutions to your challenges when you decide to take action and you are serious about doing something about it.

Partner, if you noted that you are serious about enhancing your relationship with your partner in both Secret #4 and in this section then we can focus your attention on the *"Other People"* worksheet. On the worksheet you will notice its focus is about other people. I have several questions I will ask you. These questions will guide you in your attempt to fill in your responses.

Let's look at the *"Other People"* worksheet that follows. Here are my questions: Have you ever witnessed any friends, family or acquaintances commit to a serious relationship? If yes, how did they interact with each other? How did they look at each other? How did they talk to each other? What were some of the bonding activities they did with each other? How did they act when problems occurred? And did they respect each other? Think about the time when you witnessed this. Do you remember how you felt watching them? Can you imagine yourself with your partner just as you saw others who were in a successful relationship? Now write about the encounters on the "Other People" worksheet. Also include how you felt.

Other People

Secret # 5: How to Generate a Plan

If you have never witnessed loving couples, and that is the type of relationship you want to develop, have you watched romance movies in which a character showed what appeared to be genuine love? This is truly not the same as real experiences; however, if this is what we need to get you to achieve your dreams, then try to write how you felt and what you saw on the screen.

I want you to have fun right now. Breathe in the priceless image of you and your partner acting similar to those who have had a successful partnership. Now close your eyes for a few moments and think of those images. When you are ready, open your eyes and write down any additional thoughts that come to your mind on the "*Other People*" worksheet. Would your plan be to act similar to how other successful people in relationships act? Would your plan include having conversations with people who have successful relationships?

Do you feel you are ready to continue? Great! Now we are going to probe deeper into your past relationships. It's time to move to the "*Creating My Plan*" worksheet. This worksheet consists of two categories. The categories are "*Young Me*" and "*Adult Me*". The first set of questions is based on you when you were young. Let's say age 18 and younger. The second set of questions probe into your life during your adult years. However, these questions do not pertain to your present loved one.

Think back to the days when you were a youngster, and answer these questions. When you were young did anyone ever tell you they loved you? It could have been a family member as well as other people. Did you have any serious boyfriend/girlfriend relationships? If yes, how long did the relationship last? I am asking the latter question because some people marry their childhood sweethearts. How did you feel most of the time when you were in a serious relationship? Were you beyond happy, ecstatic? Did you love this person? Did you think that maybe one day the two of you would get married? Now I want you to write the person's name, describe the relationship in detail, and how this person made you feel. Excellent! I want to say, if someone told you they loved you, you were blessed to have experienced love at such a young age. I want you to cherish those positive feelings you experienced for a few moments. Please write your responses under the *"Young Me"* section.

Creating My Plan

Young Me	Adult Me

Now let's go to the right side of the page, the *"Adult Me"* side. Remember do not include your present loved one when responding to these questions. This time respond as an adult. Has anyone ever told you they loved you? It could have been a family member as well as other people. Have you ever told anyone you loved them? What was their reaction when you said you loved them? Did you have any serious boyfriend/girlfriend relationships or marriages? If yes, how long were you involved in the relationship — for months, years? How did you feel? Were you feeling happy, ecstatic at any point in your relationship?

We need to pay a little more attention to the adult category so we can understand what type of plans we need to make. If you were in a relationship that ended, who terminated it? Why? The last question pertained to friendships as well. You have to be truthful to yourself. This answer may be one of the keys to help you to build a better relationship with your present partner. If any of the mistakes were on your part, do you want those or similar mistakes to become the reason for this relationship not to blossom? Also, if your partner left you, you need to feel secure about relationships and yourself again. Maybe one of your plans could be not to make similar mistakes in this relationship. You have to recapture your greatness.

If you are feeling some discomfort right now, hang in there. Actually write why you feel some discomfort. Now take some deep breaths. When we have the unpleasant and discomforting feelings out in the open it will be easier to move you from a planning stage to the reality stage. Take a moment to write your responses to these questions and any other thoughts about your past relationships that come to your mind on the "Adult Me" side of the page. Also include in your writing the person's name, describe the relationship in details, and how this person made you feel.

Partner, if you experienced love and affection during your lifetime, then it may not be so difficult for you to recreate this wonderful feeling for your loved one as well. I know there are other factors that come into play. However, think about it! You wrote about others who have proclaimed their love to you, and how you may have done the same towards someone else in the past. I must add, you can be the first one to let your feelings be known to your significant other, especially if he/she has difficulty expressing emotions. You can lead the way. Be the courageous one!

I have some suggestions as to how you can move your relationship with your partner along. These suggestions would involve you creating a better relationship with at least one of your family members first. Maybe this will be a little easier to do. If you are interested, answer these questions and try this approach. Have you ever thought about building your relationship with a family member — anyone except the main one we are focusing on right now? Would you consider developing your relationship with a family member first, then your partner afterwards?

If you want, you can begin by bonding with a family member. Find out, if you do not already know, some of the things you both have in common. Do things together. Call and send text messages a little more often. You must honestly want to bond with this family member. Please be truthful to yourself and respect this family member. As you bond, you can write how you feel before and after your bonding experiences. Plan to receive genuine feedback during your bonding interactions from the family member. A word of caution: I am not suggesting that you ask anyone, "How am I doing?" Your feedback should take the form of something like this: your family member is happy to hear from you and wants to include you in his/her life. Keep in mind that when you begin to reach out, this family member and others may feel startled that you want to bond with him/her. They may want to know why you have an urge to be friendly. That is to be expected. You can let your family member know that your intention is to bond more successfully with him/her and others. Comrade, please do not start with the family member whose relationship with you is the most difficult. That will entail a different type of coaching.

The family bonding approach may offer a strategy needed to help your relationship grow with your loved one as well as with others. You can observe how the family member reacts towards you. Who knows, you may want to choose to bond with another family member immediately after. This bonding approach may make it easier for you to connect with your partner because you will have had some practice in developing stronger relationship ties with people you have not connected with easily in your past. Since you will get feedback from those you bonded with, the feedback can help you to become more comfortable in pursuing your relationship with your partner. In addition the feedback can help to build your self confidence.

Since the bonding strategy can be used as a plan, here are some suggestions as to how bonding can make your relationship with your partner more gratifying. You may want to consider trying some of the following suggestions with family members first, especially if you decide to begin building your relationship with one of them. It wouldn't hurt. If you want to build your relationship with a friend you can use several of these suggestions as well. Hopefully you would want to consider these ideas with your significant other. Partner, several of these suggestions you may have already done in the past. If yes, that is great. However, I have included some proper mannerisms during male and female interactions.

The bonding suggestions offered fall under the topic or category of God, dining out, dance, sports, games, movies, and travel. Remember, you want to enjoy each other's company. You want to focus on what you can do. Keep your energy positive, and think positively. I am sure you are familiar with many of these ideas. However, during this journey it may be wise to begin doing them again. Or you may want to consider trying some of the ideas that are unfamiliar to both of you, preferably sooner than later. These suggestions are my way of helping you to spark up your relationship with things to do. Of course you could choose other activities other than the ones I suggest. The most important thing is that both of you do something together. Enjoy your lives together.

GOD:

Do both of you, one of you or neither of you, believe in God? Do both of you pray and give thanks often, sometimes, or never? If you praise God, do you praise Him together or individually? Do you feel comfortable praying together when you are at your house of worship? Have you openly seen your partner pray? If no, do you plan to make praying together one of your goals? One thing I hope is that one or both of you do not feel a need to hide from the other when praying and giving thanks to God.

If neither of you believe in God, you have something in common. Neither of you will be asking the other one to attend a house of worship. Neither of you will probably view religious television stations or have paraphernalia that makes you feel closer to God. However, be prepared when situations become unbearable; one of you may call for God's help. I have seen it happen.

Now if only one of you believes in God and attends church and prays, your relationship at some point may experience conflicts. The believer will probably spend some time in religious settings and amongst people who speak about God, while the disbeliever may feel left out or not want to be around other believers who converse about God. Or the non-believer may speak negatively about God amongst his/her family and peers who feel the same way. This opposition can cause disharmony in your relationship. I have seen it happen. Since you have conflicting views about God, this would not be a good bonding strategy for enhancing your relationship. Keep in mind maybe one of you will convert. Nonetheless, do not be dismayed; there are other bonding suggestions.

Let's focus on the idea that both of you believe in God. You have much in common. Have you agreed to attend a house of worship together? Or if each of you enjoys a specific one, you may want to alternate going to each other's preferred site. After praying at a house of worship, you can discuss the sermon of the day and reflect on how the sermon impacted each of you. This can be done during a meal at a restaurant or while eating a home cooked meal. In addition, friends and family who believe in God are most likely to be accepted around both of you, at least, when you talk about His words. With both of you believing in God, you already have a deep bond.

Partner, a conversation concerning each other's belief or disbelief in God needs to be addressed if you want harmony and stability in your relationship. Regardless of your preference, be cordial towards each other and show respect.

DINING OUT:

Earlier I mentioned dining out after attending a house of worship. However, I want to be more specific about how dining out can make the relationship richer. I am not going to focus on the types of foods you eat. Eating out often is not my suggestion. It is what you do while eating out that I feel is important to mention. Therefore this is one of several ways you can interact with each other in order to make your personal relationship a more suited one.

When you and your loved one are going to dine out, let's start with a positive attitude. One can write a cute invitation or love note. Be creative. If both of you go to the restaurant together, the male can open the car door and all other doors for the female and extend his hand to her as she exits and enters. If they are taking a bus, the male can walk out of the bus first, and then he can extend his hand to her as she exits the bus. She must accept his advances and gracefully thank him. I know this sounds like chivalry. That's okay! Remember, you are on a mission to create a richer relationship with your partner.

In terms of the meal, whoever is paying should be able to afford the food at the restaurant. In most cases it is the male paying for the meal. If the male is not married to the female, the female should be prepared to pay for her own meal — just in case. Expect to pay for the most expensive meal. Men, if the female insists on paying all or most of the time for her meal, then ask her if she considers this to be a date. Partner, it is important that both of you eat, drink and be merry.

The conversation should be positive, enjoyable and uplifting. There are so many things you can talk about while sitting at the restaurant. You can compliment your partner about their clothing, shoes, hair, perfume, after shave, etc. Some topics could be about each of your ambitions, hobbies, favorite sport or vacation planning ideas. You should feel content while in each other's company. You should feel confident enough to express your emotions if not then, at least, in the near future.

Also, the conversation should not be interrupted by cell phone calls or texting. You should agree to have the cell phones on 'vibrate' with the understanding that only emergency calls will be answered, such as the baby-sitter is calling about a child, or one of your parents has just been admitted into the hospital. I want to add; one person should not be doing all of the talking.

Be cordial towards each other and show respect. A final word; if you have some negative issues that need to be addressed, going to a restaurant is not recommended as a place to sort out your problems.

MOVIES:

Many people go on a date to the movies. Movies can offer great conversational topics. However, you cannot speak or share opinions during the movie. It is suggested that you go someplace to have a conversation about the movie you just watched. You may want to go out for a bite to eat. Regardless of how great or horrible the movie was you could have much to talk about while eating a meal. Just like on a date that involves eating, the male should open the doors and the female should thank him, etc. You want your partner to feel special, so make every effort to show it. Be cordial to each other and show respect while at the movies and dining out.

DANCE:

Now let's go with the idea of dancing. As a couple, both of you can attend dance classes together. There are many dance studios and places that offer lessons at beginner through advanced levels. Have either of you ever considered dancing lessons? You can ask your partner if he/she would like to take dancing lessons. Ballroom dancing can be so much fun, especially if both of you enjoy dancing. You can move to the rhythms of tango, salsa, disco, square dancing; and the list goes on...

The best part about attending dancing lessons is that you and your loved one will have a fun-filled activity you can do together. These classes usually show men and women how to interact with each other while dancing. Some of those moves can be used when the two of you are alone. This could be a date night both of you can look forward to having with each other. Also, you can meet other couples who enjoy this same activity. Be cordial towards each other and show respect during your dance sessions.

SPORTS:

There are so many types of sports. There has to be at least one that you can enjoy together. Anyway you look at it there are plenty of conversations that arise from participating in, or watching sports. Some people enjoy playing tennis, whilst others enjoy fishing. Presently, do you participate in a sport together? What type of sports do each of you like, if any?

One way to find out which sports are a best fit for both of you is to first view and possibly try the other's preferred sport. Another way to find a sport that suits you both is to venture into a sport unfamiliar to either of you which seems interesting enough for the two of you to try.

Maybe you will both feel more comfortable at a physical fitness center or gym. In that case, maybe weight lifting or the exercise classes may be perfect. If you and your partner are joggers, maybe you will want to increase your miles and stamina to become marathon runners in a future race. Walking in a park together can be just as enjoyable, with or without a dog.

If participating in a sport such as tennis does not work for the two of you, you can resort to watching it on a screen or going to a site to view it. You can yell, scream and shout, all in fun. Be cordial and show respect; especially if you are cheering for opposing teams.

GAMES:

There are other types of games. Games such as board games and card games can be fun. Maybe you want to play a game once a month with your partner and occasionally with friends. Do you play any particular games with your partner? If yes, how often do you play? Are other people involved sometimes, often or never?

While you are discovering yourself and each other, you may learn that one of you is more competitive than the other. If only the two of you are playing, do you win all the time? If you win all the time that is great! I am sure that is probably boosting your ego. However, do you always have to win? How do you think your partner feels to be on the losing side all the time? Is your focus to enjoy each other's company, therefore creating a meaningful relationship, or to boost your ego?

If you are always the game winner, I want you to look at the expression on the face of your partner after you've played and won three or more games in a row. Does your partner appear happy to always be the loser? Well, if you are interested in enjoying each other's company you have a couple of choices; you can let your loved one win once in a while, or you can play a game that you are both more skillful at playing. This means your partner can also win and have bragging rights just like you. What I am really saying is that it is important to be sensitive towards each other's feelings.

TRAVEL:

Travel, both local and abroad, can bring a couple closer together. Have you traveled within your country? Have you traveled abroad? Have you traveled with your partner? Traveling can offer memories - usually fond memories. There can be exceptions at times, but in general you will share great memories. If you are going on a vacation and are feuding, the chances are strong that you will continue to fight. I highly suggest that you handle any negative issues prior to going on the trip or the issues may haunt you during most of your travel time together.

You may decide with your partner to go to a wonderful place you have visited in the past. However, if you went with an ex-partner you may want to think twice. I am not saying do not go. Just think of the types of questions that may be asked, such as: who did you go with? Why did you choose this place if you were here before with someone else? Was the trip for business, pleasure or both? I suggest places neither of you have ever been to before — at least not until your relationship has evolved. New places and new experiences combined with positive attitudes are excellent ways to build your relationship with your partner.

There are different modes of transportation to get you to the location you both desire to visit. You must decide how you would like to travel to your destination. If one or both have a fear of flying or rocking on a cruise ship, then that mode of transportation is not for you. A bit of information: in terms of cruising. On a river cruise ship you feel minimal motion in the water. You can spend weeks on a riverboat cruise. People on this type of boat do not experience nearly as much rocking as on a cruise ship. I can attest to that. Your meals, entertainment and sightseeing in another land usually make a wonderful, unforgettable experience. Some riverboat cruises take up to thirty passengers; while others allow hundreds of passengers. You may want to reconsider the option of cruising. Or maybe driving, riding a train or bus is best for both of you. Regardless of your mode of transportation, be cordial and show respect towards each other during your travels.

Now let's see how we can plan a richer relationship based on the suggestions provided or any that come to your mind. The activity worksheet that follows consists of three sections. They are the following:

1. Activities You Presently Do Together.

2. Activities Each of You Would Like to Do.

3. New Activities for Two.

The *"Activities Chart"* can serve as a guide for future activities you can do together. Deciding and trying new activities can be exciting and will stimulate conversation between the two of you about your likes, dislikes and what you are willing to try. Experiencing something new can build a relationship and create a special bond. I suggest that you view the chart first to get a sense of the types of responses you would like to write. Keep in mind that filling out the activities chart can reveal how sincere you are, and the type of action you are willing to take to build your relationship. For now you are only viewing the chart. Please do not begin doing activities with your partner nor show your partner this chart yet. I will suggest when to fill out the chart and when to do activities. We are in the *"Generating Your Plans"* stage. We still have more Secrets in the relationship section that need to be covered.

Activities Chart

Activities You Presently Do Together

1.

2.

3.

Activities Each of You Would Like to Do

1.

2.

3.

New Activities for Two

1.

2.

3.

Part 2. How to Apply the Seven Secrets to Relationships

I have offered you a plethora of suggestions to help you gain a richer relationship with your partner as well as a family member and friend. Of course, you do not have to try all that were suggested; and I know there are many more I did not mention. However, at some point in time trying a suggestion or two may be all you need to give your relationship that spark.

Keep this in mind — quality time is much more valuable in a relationship than just being physically present. If you have been in the presence of someone and that person does not say a word to you, is acting as if you do not exist, or the person spends most of the time on a cell phone while in your company, that is not quality time. Now let's turn it around. An hour or more of interactive time and enjoying one another's company is pleasurable. Once again the key word is 'interactive.' I am going to exclude watching television, even though that can have some interactive moments. However, interactive video games, doing puzzles together, planning events and projects, as well as the above mentioned suggestions, will all provide quality time together.

I have to add this important note and I suppose there is no time like the present. Looking at someone else or spending much time with someone else other than your romantic partner is a sure way to lose your partner or build a level of uncertainty in your relationship. You must stay focused on your 'prize.' If you feel bored at times just refer to the activities chart or add new adventures to your list.

I am not promoting that you do everything together. The suggestions I mentioned are to help you build your personal relationship so that you have some enjoyable times together. You must do interactive activities together and share similar beliefs in order to sustain the relationship. These suggestions I have offered you can give you some foundation. We both know there will be some difficult times in your relationship, as well. When your loved one or friend thinks about the great times you have had together it will make your relationship one worth keeping. Isn't this what you want?

Now what if your partner does not want to participate in any activities with you? Or your interactions are minimal? Then you may have a problem. You will need to have a serious discussion to find out why you should not be engaged in activities together and why you are not spending quality time with each other. Since you want a more meaningful relationship, you will both have to put some time into making it work. Fond memories and enjoying each other's company come from doing things together. Now the question is what type of relationship does your partner want?

One important thing you must keep in mind is that people react differently and feel differently towards you. Also, there are different types of love and relationships- motherly, fatherly, sisterly, brotherly, spousal, occasional friend, platonic, girlfriend and boyfriend.

Is there a possibility the person may not feel the same way about you at all? If that happens and you have already put your emotions out there, it's ok. It's ok! You will have expressed what you felt and do not have to wonder any more. You have developed what I am going to call 'emotional courage.' So you may feel upset for a little while; however you should feel relieved to have expressed and done what was in your heart.

At this point you can continue the relationship knowing how the other person feels at the present time. Your other choice is to terminate the relationship. I would urge you to continue the relationship for at least a little longer. I am going to tell you why. Maybe your significant other has difficulty bonding and expressing their love, or your partner is experiencing a similar relationship challenge like you are.

Maybe if you express your feelings you will become a role model for your partner. It could be that your partner is looking at your sincerity, and after a short period of time he/she will feel comfortable enough to react with less of a defensive attitude. So becoming a role model and using a role model approach can serve as a plan to develop your relationship as well. Personally I think if the latter occurred it would be a double reward. Not only would you break your own fear cycle but you would also help your loved one do the same.

Do you think it is possible that your loved one feels insecure or shy around you, or vice versa? Well, if that is the case, communication seems like a strategy you may want to seriously consider. Partner, if there is no communication, there will be no advancement in your relationship.

I have offered three types of approaches you can use for generating a plan to create a richer relationship with your loved one. The plans are in the categories of bonding, acting as a role model, and communicating with your loved one. You may want to consider more than one plan for optimum results. Maybe you can come up with a few plans that you feel will work best for you and your partner. You decide the approach. Remember to take into account factors such as timing, location, likes and dislikes. Regardless of the plan you choose it is of utmost importance to love and respect one's self. Go to www.transformationplus.com for 4 methods to maintain a relationship.

Have you come up with a plan to write on the "*My Plan*" worksheet? You may want to refer to prior worksheets, such as "*Creating My Plan*" and the "*Activities Chart*" from this Secret, and the "*My Goals*" worksheet in Secret # 4. Those exercises can guide you towards how you can attain your goals. Partner, a few detailed plans are all you need.

My Plan

1.

2.

3.

4.

SELF-DISCOVERY CHECKPOINT:

It is time for another Self-discovery Check. Since the first check you envisioned your dreams, created goals and generated a plan of action. Let's find out how you are feeling right now. Remember we want you to become more successful in your personal life. So answer these questions very truthfully, as they pertain to your personal relationships.

STRESS LEVEL ASSESSMENT

1. **What is your present stress level from 1 through 10? Please circle your response.**

(1 = very low stress level, 5 = some stress, 10 = very high stress level).

Stress Number Line

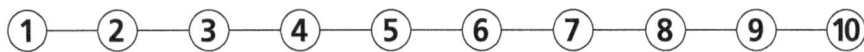

2. **What stresses are you experiencing right now, if any? Explain.**

3. **Based on the Stress vs. Success balance beams:**
   i. Which of the 3 diagrams best represents you?

      a. Stress is overpowering

      b. I can succeed/ Success is possible

      c. Balanced

   ii. Which diagram best describes how you feel when you are involved with your partner?

      a. Stress is overpowering

      b. I can succeed/ Success is possible

      c. Balanced

Stress vs. Success

Stress — Success Joy
Stress is over powering (a)

or

Success Joy — Stress
I can succeed/ Success is possible (b)

Balanced (c)

Part 2. How to Apply the Seven Secrets to Relationships

4. **Do you feel you can achieve success in this relationship?**
   Yes ___ **No** ___

   i. If yes, in what ways do you feel you can be successful?

   ii. If no, why not?

5. **How would you rank your energy level on a scale of 1 through 10? Please circle your response.**

   (1= very low, 5= some energy, 10= very high)

   Energy Level Number Line

Secret # 6: Discover How to Timeline Your Tasks

So let's get your timeline in order. One possible plan mentioned was to build your relationship with at least one family member first, then develop the relationship with your partner. If you decided to build a stronger tie with a few people, I do not suggest that you enhance your relationship with everyone at the same time. You could — but if you want to learn from the experience it would probably be wiser to focus on one person at a time.

Choosing bonding activities, which was a plan suggested earlier, has to fit both of your personalities and schedules. For instance, you should not take evening dance lessons if one of you has a work schedule that fluctuates during evening hours. Then you must consider other options. This may mean you both have to take some time to come up with a new activity that fits both of your schedules.

Also, your locations and the availability of the person need to be considered in your timeline. If your loved one is overseas or in another state, you have to wait until you see this person again. It may take weeks or months! Continuing a long distance relationship by telephone, email and mail may be the only means of communication, at least until your partner returns home.

If you are planning to propose marriage, making reservations to be at a specific place has to fit both of your time schedules. Pricey places and items that show affection are great! However, they may take time to reserve or purchase. If you want to start a family, that usually involves finances. We know buying items such as disposable diapers and baby furniture is expensive. You may want to decide when having children is more affordable and when it best suits your lifestyles.

On the "*Timeline*" worksheet that follows, you will be asked to write your principal task and mini tasks- those ideas you want to accomplish. The mini tasks can prepare and lead you towards your principal task. You should add next to each task the date or time frame you feel you would need to implement each task. Partner, this part of your journey involves when you plan to take action. It would be even better if you wrote specifically how you plan to go about accomplishing each task. Along the way some of your ideas or the time frame may have to be altered and new tasks may have to be added. Regardless, the timeline gives us structure as to how and when you can approach your objectives.

The following is an example of one principal task and six mini tasks with a time frame: However you can use your "Generating A Plan" worksheets, in the prior chapter, to help you make detailed plans that can yield success more quickly.

Principal Task:

Marry my partner. Date to be accomplished: 1 year.

Mini Tasks:

a) Decide wedding style - 1 months.

b) Choose wedding party - 2 months

c) Reserve ceremony and reception venues - 3 months

d) Meet with officiate to discuss plans for ceremony – 6 months

e) Finalize guest list - 8 months

f) Order wedding favors - 9 months

Months	1	2	3	4	5	6	7	8	9	10	11	12
Tasks	a	b	c			d		e	f			

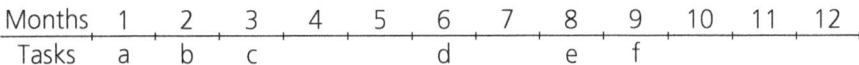

Secret # 6: Discover How to Timeline Your Tasks

Now try to create a timeline of what you wish to accomplish, and when you feel it could be completed. Create a schedule as best as you can with the intention of meeting those obligations you have set as your plans. You can refer to the *Timeline* number line in Part 1 Secret # 6 for additional guidance.

Timeline

1. Principal Task:

How I plan to accomplish it:

Date to be accomplished:

a. Mini Task:

How I plan to accomplish it:

Date to be accomplished:

b. Mini Task:

How I plan to accomplish it:

Date to be accomplished:

c. Mini Task:

How I plan to accomplish it:

Date to be accomplished:

Months	1	2	3	4	5	6	7	8	9	10	11	12
Tasks												

Begin doing all of the things you wrote on your timeline. Start accomplishing your mini tasks. If you feel you need to add more tasks, do so. You may want to refer to the worksheets in Secret # 5, "*How to Generate a Plan.*" Partner, now is the time to fill out the "*My Activities*" list located in Secret # 5 with your partner, and engage in some of the activities both of you wrote together and decided upon doing.

When all of your mini tasks are achieved, you should feel ready to accomplish your final objective. You are already achieving your dreams. Think about it. You accomplished your minis. Now you are ready to achieve your ultimate dream. This is when you can look in the mirror and practice what you want to say to your loved one, at least a day or two prior to the big date.

Secret # 7: You Have Arrived! Now Live Your Dreams!

Partner, it's time to achieve your ultimate relationship dream! Yes, it is time to live your dreams and make them a reality. You have spent time rediscovering yourself, making goals, thinking of engaging actions that would allow your partner to see your seriousness and sincerity. You should feel ready to achieve your ultimate dream. So, go up to your loved one and proclaim your love. Because it's time to express your love, show it, be the best partner ever.

Say it, Do it! Proclaim it! Sharing your love with your partner — PRICELESS.

Congratulations, action-taker, you are doing it! You have unleashed your greatness from within, and you are living your dream. Be ready to make more progress. The next part of the book focuses exclusively on careers. As you read and do exercises to enhance your career you will acquire more opportunities- for success .

SELF-DISCOVERY CHECKPOINT:

Thus far we have spent time together doing a few Self-discovery Checks. We focused on your strengths as well as your life's problems. We envisioned, created goals and a plan, made a timeline and you did what you set out to do. Let's find out how you are feeling right now. We are engaged in this because I want you to realize how successful you have become in a personal challenge you faced. So once again answer these questions very truthfully.

STRESS LEVEL ASSESSMENT

1. **What is your present stress level from 1 through 10? Please circle your response.**

(1 = very low stress level, 5 = some stress, 10 = very high stress level).

Stress Number Line

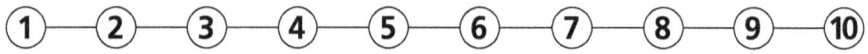

2. **What stresses are you experiencing right now, if any? Explain.**

3. **Based on the Stress vs. Success balance beams:**

    i. Which of the 3 diagrams best represents you?

    a. Stress is overpowering

    b. I can succeed/ Success is possible

    c. Balanced

    ii. Which diagram best describes how you feel when you are involved with your partner?

    a. Stress is overpowering

    b. I can succeed/ Success is possible

    c. Balanced

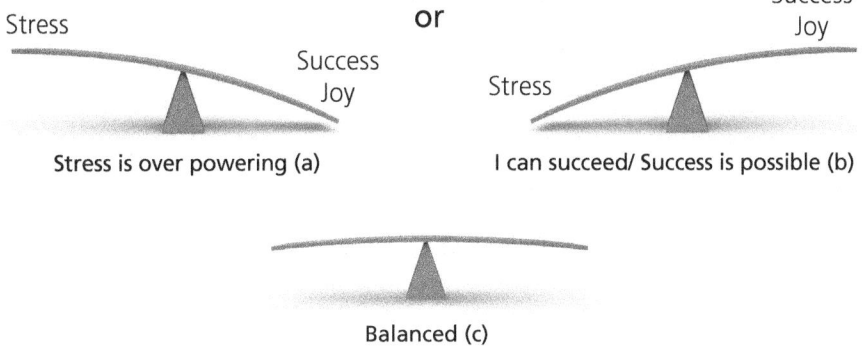

Secret # 7: You Have Arrived! Now Live Your Dreams!

4. Do you feel you have achieved success?
   Yes ___ No ___

   i. If yes, in what ways do you feel you can be successful?

   ii. If no, why not?

5. How would you rank your energy level on a scale of 1 through 10? Please circle your response.

   (1 = very low, 5 = some energy, 10 = very high)

   Energy Level Number Line

   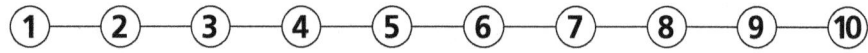

Your self discovery check results should be great, especially because you completed your tasks and had success learning new and wonderful things about yourself. Do you feel awesome? Do you feel uplifted? Now that you have measured your energy and stress vs. success levels, I would like you to look at all of these charts from the beginning of the relationship process to the end. Noting the changes and when they occurred may help you when you are ready to take on your next quest for personal growth and success.

As you view all of the worksheets, did you notice a difference in yourself in the beginning and at the end of your journey? If so, when did the change occur? Your most important challenge may have been to build your self confidence so that you could express your true feelings to your partner and develop a richer relationship. If yes, when did you feel your self confidence change? Did you notice a change in your stress vs. success levels? What changes happened along the way; and when did these changes take place? Can you pinpoint the phase when you felt successful? Or do you feel success came when you were at the end zone, when you completed your journey? Believe me, the most important thing right now is that you feel successful and that you have recaptured your greatness.

Congratulations partner, you set out to do what was important to you.

Part 3

How to Apply the Seven Secrets to Career Advancement

"Your work is to discover your work and then with all your heart to give yourself to it."

Buddha

Careers

Most of us have to work in order to pay bills, eat, drink and have a place to rest our heads. We also need to have money to enjoy the finer things in life. Many people work so they can afford to do all of these things. There are people who love their jobs, people who hate their jobs and others who are somewhere in the middle.

Where do you stand? Do you work at your job just to receive a paycheck? What vision do you have of yourself in the next two, five and ten years? These are just a few of the questions I would like you to seriously think about as we probe into your professional life.

Since I mention career advancement quite often in Part 1 of the book, I decided to devote a section of this book to careers. Most, if not all, people who stay at their job for decades desire a good pension. Usually better pensions come with higher paying salaries. I can coach you in your quest for upward mobility at your job. I believe you want to be recognized as an excellent worker who deserves more than you are presently offered. If yes, be ready to embark on a journey; however, in the long run think of all of the positive benefits — more money and a better retirement lifestyle.

The *"Seven Secrets to Achieve Your Dreams"* design has been used in this book to guide those who are experiencing professional and personal challenges. As we focus the attention on career advancement, I will ask you several questions to help you to explore your possibilities and to find solutions. As your partner, I can help you ponder, envision and engage in some role-playing in order to help you make decisions crucial to your professional growth.

Part 3. How to Apply the Seven Secrets to Career Advancement

Partner, do you have only a few more years until retirement and want to remain at your job? Do you have the skills and drive to move up the corporate ladder? Do you feel bored with what you are presently doing at the job and have what it takes to make the business more profitable? If your response was yes to at least one of these questions, or if you want to be able to do any of the above, we have work to do. So let's get you started on your journey to professional success.

Since we may encounter some unpleasant periods in this section, and I want you to feel at ease, I will suggest taking power breaks. The power breaks will consist of drinking a cool glass of water or a hot, minty, herbal tea, deep breathing exercises, standing up, stretching out, and inhaling the aroma of a scented candle, as you have done in previous sections. It would be great if you have small pictures of yourself as a child and as an adult handy. Partner, career advancement will not be an easy task, so get ready to embark on an adventure. I will coach you and be your cheerleader during your trials and tribulations. You will be asked to write information in worksheets and number lines in order to keep you focused on your task for career advancement. Are you ready to begin? Great!

Secret #1:
How to Identify Your Strengths

Using the *"Seven Secrets to Achieve Your Dreams"* design that was revealed in Part 1 of this book, I want to begin by asking you questions about your strengths as they pertain to your work ethics. Think of what the people at your job say about you. How do they positively label you? I know labeling someone is not always a good thing, but we have to recapture your power from within by first identifying what powers you possess.

Here are a few questions I would like you to answer. Remember, we are focusing solely on your positive strengths. Do you like the type of work you do? Do you hand in your work on time? Do you participate in conferences and seminars that enhance your skills? Do you show passion and excitement when working? Well, if you answered yes to these questions you are on a clear path to success. Please continue on this positive path and focus on what you can do to achieve your vision.

It is time to look at the *"My Strengths"* worksheet page that follows. Place the child and adult pictures of you above the page but do not attach them to the page. Let's start by thinking about some of your positive youthful characteristics on the *"Young Me"* side of the page. I will help you to begin the thought process. In school, when you were 18 and younger, did you complete your homework assignments on or before time? Were you an "A" above average student? Did you take pride in how your work looked? Was your work neat? Did you enjoy presenting your school work in front of others? Did classmates look up to you and want you to be in their project and study group? Did you pay attention to details when you did your projects? Now write about the positive work ethics you had as a youngster.

My Strengths

Young Me	Adult Me

Secret #1: How to Identify Your Strengths

You can use several of these same questions and answer them based on your present job performance in the "Adult Me" section of the chart. Just to add a few more questions, have you had any job promotions or been selected to do special projects? The more positives you write about yourself the better equipped you will be, especially if you will need a positive energy boost at a later time. Partner, I will suggest that you revisit this section if you do not score well on your assessments as we move from one Secret to the next.

Secret # 2:
How to Survey Life's Problems

In the beginning of the book you were asked to *"Survey Your Life's Problems."* If you wrote that you want to advance in your career and/or earn more money, continue reading. I hope you are motivated enough to take on this challenge. However, if this is not an area in need of improvement or you are not ready to take on this challenge then you are more than welcome to share this information with someone else or read this at a time when you feel it would be beneficial to you.

Now, about your life's problems; here are a few questions. Do you complete your work-related tasks after the deadlines? Are you unsure of what you should be doing? Are you qualified for upward mobility positions at the job, but others are getting the positions you know you are qualified to receive? Do you dislike the work you do? Do you dislike your co-workers or the bosses? Are you being bullied or taken advantage of at your job? If possible, would you prefer to leave the job and seek employment elsewhere?

I know I asked several questions — and I still have a few more. Using the *"Life's Problems"* worksheet, we will focus on you at two different stages in your life. The first stage would be of you up to the age of 18, and the second stage is you as an adult. Now take the two photographs of yourself, one of you as a child and the other as an adult and place the pictures above the worksheet without attaching them.

Let's probe into the types of problems you faced during your youthful days. You can begin to write your responses on the *"Young Me"* side of the chart that follows. What type of relationship did you have with your teachers? Were you always disciplined because you did not hand in your work on time or because you did not follow directions? Did you have to stay in class during social activities to complete your assignments? Did your peers reject you when it was time to choose study groups because they knew you would not do your portion of the assigned projects? Were your grades usually failures? Did you get left back? Did you hate going to school? Were you picked on by bullies? When you were given chores to do at home were you irresponsible? Did your family members pick on you or not include you in activities? The last set of questions are not related to school, however your responses give some clues about your relationship with people who were around you often, and if you were cooperative in terms of responsibilities and tasks. Remember to write your responses on the youth side of the page.

Life's Problems

Young Me	Adult Me

Secret # 2: How to Survey Life's Problems

Now let's delve into your adulthood. How are things presently at work? Remember we are focusing on the problems you are facing. Do you have problems saving money? Do you have problems investing money? Are you unable to earn a decent salary? Comrade, what type of relationship do you have with your boss? How are you treated by your boss and co-workers? Are you not receiving credit for excellent work you have done? Do co-workers and the boss disrespect you and the work you do? Based on your career goal, what has kept you from achieving your goal in the past? Do you feel these job-related problems are solvable and if not, why? Are you discontent when you are at work? Is this discontent affecting you when you are heading towards your job each day and when you are going home? Are people bullying you? Are you being taken for granted? Do you take care of your responsibilities at home and do you complete your home projects? Once again the last set of questions are not job-related however it can give a clue or two about how you handle yourself around others, and how you handle responsibilities.

Since surveying one's problems is, in my opinion, the most unpleasant section, let's stop and take a power break. Breathe in and breathe out. Once again, breathe in and breathe out. You may want to drink some cool water or a hot, relaxing tea right now. If you want to stretch out for a moment this may be a good time to do so. Are you ready to continue? Excellent!

Surveying your life's problems is designed to help you learn exactly what needs to be accomplished, what may be holding you back, and what elements are blocking you. Our objective is to help you acknowledge what you need to focus on in order to obtain success. Please, and I am going to repeat the word please again, yes, please do not place blame on someone else because you are facing a problem. If you blame others, you may feel there is nothing you need to do or can do to alter your situation; also you may feel no true need to make life better for yourself.

Start answering the questions pertaining to your adult life on the "*Adult Me*" side of the page. Partner, you can learn much about yourself by answering these types of questions. I know the answers are not going to be uplifting. However, we cannot get to the root of your problems until you express what is truly going on with you. You may have a few of your own thoughts you may want to add.

SELF-DISCOVERY CHECKPOINT

This is a good time to do a Self-discovery Check. We focused on your strengths as well as your life's problems. Let's find out how you are feeling right now. We want you to become more successful in your professional life. Remember you can refer to the "*How to Evaluate Your Self-discovery Check*" in Part 1 of the book, to obtain information about scoring, as well as learn when it is recommended to proceed to the next chapter. So answer these questions very truthfully.

STRESS LEVEL ASSESSMENT

1. **What is your present stress level from 1 through 10? Please circle your response.**

(1 = very low stress level, 5 = some stress, 10 = very high stress level).

Stress Number Line

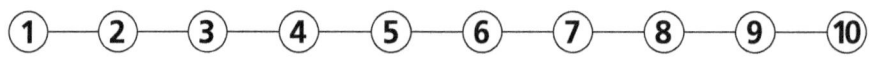

2. **What stresses are you experiencing right now, if any? Explain.**

3. **Based on the Stress vs. Success balance beams that follow:**

    i. Which of the 3 diagrams best represents you?

    a. Stress is overpowering

    b. I can succeed/ Success is possible

    c. Balanced

    ii. Which diagram best describes how you feel when you interact with your boss?

    a. Stress is overpowering

    b. I can succeed/ Success is possible

    c. Balanced

    iii. Which diagram best describes how you feel when you interact with your co-workers?

    a. Stress is overpowering

    b. I can succeed/ Success is possible

    c. Balanced

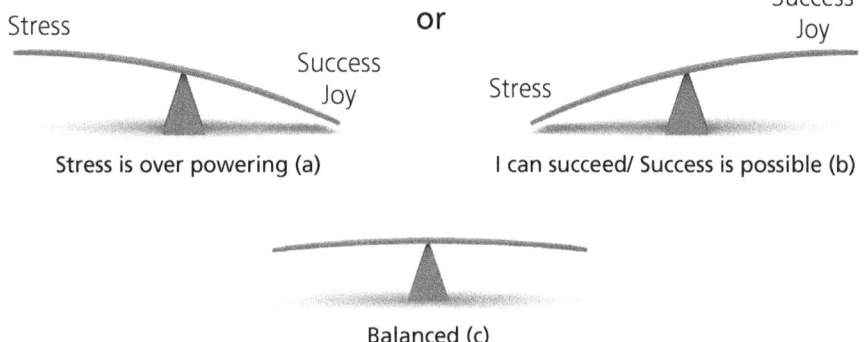

Secret # 2: How to Survey Life's Problems

4. **Do you feel you can achieve success in the near future?**
   Yes ___ No ___

   i. If yes, in what ways do you feel you can be successful?

   ii. If no, why not?

5. **How would you rank your energy level on a scale of 1 through 10? Please circle your response.**

   (1= very low, 5= some energy, 10= very high)

   Energy Level Number Line

   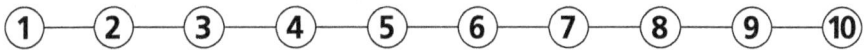

Secret # 3:
Discover How to Envision Your Dreams

Using Secret # 3, we are going to envision you at your perfect job, doing what it is that will make you feel content. What do I mean by envisioning your dreams? People tend to have dreams or thoughts of something they are interested in. However they have not pursued that thought or vision yet. In other words, you have dreams of yourself doing something you enjoy and getting paid for it. We will engage in an envisioning exercise. But first I would like you to refer to the "*My Vision*" worksheet for a moment. Place the adult picture of yourself in the top of the page and write your name below the picture. Partner, your imagination is the key component in this secret.

Now I want you to spend this precious time *re-imagining your life*. I want to point out how important it is to have your own specific vision, and not a vision that someone else has for you. You may feel the need to start out by deciding what you do not want to do in order to get a better sense of what you do want to accomplish.

Now let's begin an envisioning exercise. I want you to take a few deep breaths. Inhale, now exhale. Once again inhale, now exhale. *Re-imagine your life.* While you are imagining, put a smile on your face. Imagine yourself at the job you yearn to have. Let's get more intense. Think of what you would like to do at your job. Who is with you? What are you and your co-workers conversing about? What are you wearing? And what is your title and position at your job? If your new position entails extra hours and the type of paperwork you prefer to do, partner, do you see yourself feeling content while taking on these responsibilities? Do you see yourself comfortable being in a position with more business accountability and more money?

My last question is - do you see your ingenious job-related plans in action? Take a few more deep breaths. Inhale, now exhale. Again inhale, exhale. As you continue to think for a few more moments, close your eyes. Enjoy your vision, your vision of success. You are closer to success than what you think. Now open your eyes and write your fantastic work-related vision. While you are writing be happy and continue to smile.

My Vision

1.

2.

3.

Secret # 3: Discover How to Envision Your Dreams

Secret # 4: How to Create Your Goals

Are you feeling energized and ready to create your goals? Excellent! Partner, you just envisioned and wrote down your new job title and/or the new type of responsibilities you would like to have at your workplace. Now it is time to create some goals. Goals are those things you want to accomplish. The things you are aiming for in your life - your hopes, your aspirations. I have some questions I would like you to answer. Do you want to continue working on your career vision? Do you feel it is important to act as soon as possible, or wait? Are you considering changing job sites or positions? Use your "*My Visions*" worksheet from Secret # 3 to assist you in creating your goals.

Comrade, has your vision shifted? If you answered yes, then what is the shift, and why has it occurred? Do you want to be acknowledged and receive monetary payment when you come up with innovative ideas? Do you know your monetary worth at the company? Do you want to stop working endless hours? Do you want to be one of the top employees, or an employer? Are you interested in winning the Award of the Year? Do you want to participate in or create special tasks and activities? Do you want to work from home or in an office setting? I have asked you quite a few questions. Now I would like you to measure your level of seriousness about the next question. On a scale from 1 to 5, how serious are you about achieving your career-minded vision?

Circle your response.

1 = not serious

2 = somewhat serious

3 = average

4 = serious

5 = very serious

As your partner, I suggest that we may have to shape and reshape your goals as we move along. That's okay! Maybe you are ready to gain more status at a job, do different or extra tasks. We need to do a little more probing. You need to know exactly what is required of you, what tasks need to be accomplished and what resources are available to you. You may want a position and you find out that the position entails assignments that are unfamiliar to you or tasks that you do not enjoy doing. So find out as much about the position as possible.

Remember, I am your partner. I will guide you through your goal-reaching process. Now, what goals do you wish to achieve? What is your first goal, your second goal; and why are you choosing these goals? As you are thinking of at least four goals, I want to ask you a few more questions. Are these realistic goals? Do you feel you will be able to reach the first goal in a timely manner? Take some time to think and to write your response to these questions on the *"My Goals"* page. Allow the previous questions and *"My Visions"* worksheet in Secret # 3 to help you come up with some general goals. After writing your goals I want you to review them one more time.

My Goals

1.

2.

3.

4.

5.

Secret # 5 How to Generate A Plan

This is great! You have written some goals so now you are probably ready to begin to generate a plan. This is the next step towards making your career-minded vision become a reality. You must decide on the approach, the plan, you will use to make your goals become a reality - how you will go about getting what you want. The plan you create should help you achieve the goals you set for yourself.

Generating a plan can make it possible for you to have more money in your pockets. If you inherited money through a family "will" it is wise to think of how you plan to spend it. Do you plan to invest a portion of that money in a dream to start your own company? Do you plan to save that money until you retire or for a rainy day? Or would the money you inherited be used to pay bills or debts? Some people spend it on cars, travel, partying, etc. It would be wise to take some time to make a plan.

If you plan to retire within 7 years, do you plan to work a side job at a different company to earn extra income to save towards your retirement? Do you plan to go for an executive position at your present job? Or do you plan to do extra tasks at work to increase your pension during your last few years before you retire? I highly suggest you speak with financial consultants and have consultations with them about pension plan options.

I have two types of questions I will ask you pertaining to your career plans at your present job. However, before we do this I want you to take a quick look at the *"My Plans Part A"* page and then return to this section to read more about it. On the *"My Plans Part A"* page note that there are two segments. One segment refers to "Other

People" and the second segment pertains to "Self."

Now let's focus on the *"Other People"* segment first. The following questions pertain to what you observed at the job in regards to co-workers. Here are my questions regarding "Other People." Have you seen other people at your job advance to higher ranks? Has anyone recently received the position you had your eyes on? Do you know how long theses co-workers have been at the job and the amount of experience they had at other similar jobs? Have you observed their work ethic? For example, do they hand in their work prior to deadlines, have excellent attendance, come up with some innovative ideas and display a zealous attitude? Think about what they do that makes them stand apart from others. What have you witnessed? Have you noticed a difference as to how the boss interacts with those employees to whom he/she has given the higher ranking positions or extra paying side jobs? How do co-workers interact with bosses and other co-workers? How do they spend their lunch time? Are they taking long, enjoyable, personal lunch breaks? Or do they work partially during their lunch time? What do you feel is the key to their success?

Partner, please do not spend time saying all of them are the boss's favorites. This could be a possibility, just like teacher's pets exist in school. However, try to look beyond that. If you do not look beyond the thought that everyone is a favorite and you are not, you do not have a chance to achieve your dreams. It would seem that you already feel defeated in your quest. If this is how you feel, you still have choices. Look for another job, stay at the present job feeling you will never get ahead, or aspire for upward mobility. I suggest that you should stay, at least a little while longer at your job, and obtain clarity as to how people are moving ahead.

Also in terms of observing co-workers, have you noticed any of them leaving immediately after their work shift is over to go to a second job so they can earn extra income? If so, what type of positions do they have at your work place? Do they have a good or poor relationship with the boss?

One thing I must say is that I do not advocate people compromising their dignity or pride. Take some time to write those observations you have made concerning co-workers in the *"Other People"* section of the worksheet.

My Plans Part A

Other People	Self

Now let us spend some time on the *"Self"* segment of the page. This segment allows you to ponder about what you do at work, and how co-workers and bosses react to you. Remember we are trying to come up with plans of action to get you the career success you desire. Are you arriving at work on time? Do you leave work as soon as the official work day is over? If yes, is it to earn money by working at a second job? Do you ask for extensions for work-related projects? Are other people in your same job division handing in their work ahead of you? How are other people reacting to your work and ideas? Do you share your information with the right people who are in a position to offer you advancement or salary increases? Are you respected at the job, or are you almost invisible? Are you willing to acknowledge and work on personal changes that need to be made in order for you to become successful? Do you feel you can rely on a co-worker who would be able to mentor or assist you? Do you have friends who are familiar with the type of work you do and can offer you suggestions? I asked the last question because you may feel you cannot rely or trust co-workers. Have you spoken with your co-worker friends who retired and asked them how they are managing their finances?

Partner, you want to unleash your greatness from within. This greatness will be unleashed when you explore what needs to be changed, and devote your time to making the changes. So write your responses and any thoughts that come to mind about you at work in the "Self" section.

I need to add something: you may soon feel the need to revisit this section — maybe you want to stop at this point, go to work for a few days, observe the workers and monitor your personal work habits. Doing this may help you to answer the questions more accurately. Keep in mind that you may want to add to or change your responses. Afterwards I want you to note your initial responses in this section.

See if the initial responses you wrote are the same or different from what you wrote after you spent at few days at work.

Partner, since you want to make some professional changes I would like you to start by imagining yourself engaged in a new action plan, because the ultimate responses and gestures come from within. You can find solutions to your challenges when you decide on a plan and take action. For example, if you seek a more prestigious position you need to think of yourself involved in tasks that are related to the prestigious job. In order to accomplish your objectives, imagine role-playing your interaction with your co-workers and boss. Picture your boss offering you the position you desire, as well as a salary increase. Then see yourself in motion doing the specific plans you hope to accomplish.

If one of your objectives is to complete a project before the deadline, then your action plan can be to work a longer work day with a dynamic team, give and receive advice, and hand the boss the work about two days ahead of time. This could be your plan. Think about how you would feel if you really did what you set out to do. In addition to completing the assignment, you would have earned positive recognition from your boss and co-workers, therefore accomplishing a personal and professional milestone.

If you desire to make more money, what plan would you propose to earn it? Can you see yourself engaged in the strategy you are committing to do? Do you feel your plan will ultimately lead you to your success? Do you feel there is a chance for advancement if you decide to use that approach? Would the best people you have in mind be capable of assisting you, be available and be willing to work with you? Partner, your plan will take time, energy and help from others. You may want to include something in your plan that will get your boss's attention. It could be a project that provides efficiency or increased productivity for the job. Do you plan to take a job-related course so that you are more knowledgeable in your field?

There are other factors that you may want to consider while creating your plan of action, such as your passion, ambition and your body language. Your passion and ambition can get you where you want to be. Keep in mind that your body language and the way you express your thoughts to others reveal quite a bit. People can detect when you are genuine. So exhibiting your passion and how you interact are important. Whatever type of job you have, there is usually a way to impress your boss. Do you plan to change how you interact with your boss and co-workers?

On the other hand, will your plan be of a more basic type, such as better attendance and meeting your deadlines on time? Are you willing to sacrifice some of your free time to achieve your vision? Advancement usually requires some form of sacrifice, so what do you want to change and/or fix in order to obtain your career-minded vision?

Partner, you may feel uncomfortable saying and doing things that you are not accustomed to doing or saying. If you have a proposal you want to submit would you feel shy, fearful or anxious presenting it? One suggested plan to work through those uncomfortable feelings is to take a few deep breaths; think of pleasant thoughts, such as receiving the raise you may obtain in the near future; and practice your script while looking in the mirror the day before your presentation. You may also want to say some positive statements to yourself prior to going into a meeting or speaking with your boss. As little as that may seem, you may need to put that in your plan, making positive statements to self. In addition, you may want to consider corresponding with a mentor. The mentor and you can role-play some work-related scenarios. Please do not pay attention to people who stand in your way of progress. And do not neglect personal responsibilities.

Having success in your career and then letting your personal life go downhill can lead to other problems. Earlier I offered coaching for people interested in developing a richer personal relationship. When you become successful in your career and already have a great relationship with your partner, you do not want to turn around and discover that you need relationship coaching in order to enhance your relationship with a loved one. Do not worry, I will keep you on track and remind you of your mission and its possible effects on other aspects of your life. Remember, you are not alone.

I want you to think of this as a fantastic time in your life. You are ready to take action. You want something bigger and greater for yourself, and you have started the process. Imagine in the future you will become someone's role model.

Partner, you must feel comfortable with your plan of action. Basically, what I am saying is that no one should tell you what you have to do. People can make suggestions, but as an action-taker, it is you that has to be there for yourself the entire time. Your supporters may not be allowed to be in your presence when you present your one of a kind proposal to your boss.

Regardless of your goals and plans you generate, you can not slack off at your job. I strongly advise against starting to take action, only to suddenly stop. That would not work to your advantage. Do you want to send mixed messages to your boss? For example, for two months you are a dynamic worker, sharing innovative ideas and leading a special projects team; then you change into an invisible, uncaring person who hands in work late. That's not a good idea. There is no chance of advancement coming your way, so try your best to stick to your plan. You never know who is watching or reading the material you produce. Also, you never know when the opportunity will come your way or from whom it may come. So, no slacking off.

Probably now is a good time to write about four plans on the "*My Plans Part B*" chart. You may want to review the statements you wrote in the "*My Goals*" worksheet in Secret # 4, also the "*Other People*" and "*Self*" worksheets in the current Secret, to help you come up with a plan of action. On the following chart include your reason for deciding each plan. If you are self-employed and you have no plans for a promotion then there is no need to write on the following worksheet.

For 5 ways to obtain a job go to www.transformationplus.com.

My Plans Part B

I plan to do the following:

1.

Why?

2.

Why?

3.

Why?

4.

Why?

5.

Why?

Secret # 6:
Discover How to Timeline Your Tasks

You have come a long way. So now that you have your plan of action, a timeline is a great tool to help you move at a certain pace. Also the timeline can allow you to see your road more clearly because you know you want to accomplish specific objectives at specific times. We want your career plans to move hand in hand within the timeframe. Also we want your plans to be achievable during the time frame you create.

Partner, I hope you do not plan to finish reading this book then go to work feeling you can accomplish everything in a day or two. It takes time. You have to make some changes in your lifestyle. Also, your boss has to change the way he/she perceives you. This cannot be done overnight. In addition, if you changed quickly and the boss acknowledges the change, then he/she needs to find out if this is a new you or just a temporary you. On a personal note, if you have a spouse and/or children timing is also a factor. You have to consider the best time to venture into new tasks without upsetting your family's lifestyle. And under no circumstances do we want you to fall apart because you were too eager and did everything at a too-rapid pace.

Keep in mind timelines may also require prerequisites. You may have a managerial position in mind. This position may require you to present some innovative ideas. However, if you leave work immediately after the work day is over while your co-workers stay a little later to hand in their dynamic project, you may have to change your schedule and begin to stay late one or two days per week to think of, develop, and implement a creative project that the boss would like. So, not only are you creating a special project and showing your capabilities, you are spending extra time working as well. On a personal note if you have little children, a babysitter may be required.

There is another thing about timelines that must be considered. Do you feel this is the right time to put the plan in action? When would you like to begin and when would you like to achieve your objective? Is your boss going to be around to see your progress or will he/she be out of town most of the time? Do you foresee any problems as you are trying to accomplish your dreams within a reasonable amount of time? If yes, what problem do you foresee; and how can you work around it? A few more questions for you, Partner. How much time do you want to invest in making your vision a reality? And at what pace do you plan to move: slow, medium or rapid pace?

In terms of career advancement, it may take three to six months for your mini task to be accomplished and recognized. Mini tasks should not be taken lightly because these tasks require you to perform several duties. Principal tasks may take a year or more. Taking job-related courses may be something you may want to consider. Some courses take six months to a year to complete. Since much of your future accomplishments can be based on how your work is presently rated, do your homework. Learn about the budget and any positions that may become available in the future. As I mentioned before, it is going to take some time for your boss to change his/her attitude towards you. Also a new position may not become available as soon as you would like. Expect challenges; however your timeline will give you direction so that you will know when to take on the next task. Bottom line — you want to experience minimal or no chaos and confusion because you know what you want to do and when to pursue it.

We are in our final planning phase. So keep in mind that some plans may have to be altered. If some of them have to be extended or new ones may have to be added, it's okay! Next to each plan write the time span which you are giving yourself to accomplish it. Your principal task will take you the longest amount of time to accomplish because it is generally a bigger vision or requires more on your part. Your mini tasks can be the 3-month action plans needed to get to that long-term objective you are excited about achieving.

The timeline gives us structure as to how we can approach your objectives. An example of one principal task could be the following:

Although you want a higher-ranking position, you want the boss to recognize your positive efforts and contributions at the job. This dream can take more than one year. Please note this plan is written only as an example.

1. Principal Task
Higher ranking position
Date to be accomplished: **18 months**

Some mini tasks could be as follows:

a. Mini Task
Stay at work late for two days a week.
You can start this within **2 months**

b. Mini Task
Research what is needed at the job for efficiency and productivity purposes.
Start immediately and have information within **3 months**

c. Mini Task
Create a project. Begin this task after you have completed your research
Date to be accomplished: **6 months**

d. Mini Task
Prepare presentation. Date to be accomplished: **7 months**

e. Mini Task
Show presentation. Date to be accomplished: **8 months**

f. Mini Task
Implement your project at work. Date to be accomplished: **9 months**

g. Mini Task
Oversee productivity and effectiveness of project. Date to be accomplished: **12 months**

Months	1	2	3	4	5	6	7	8	9	10	11	12	13	14	15	16	17	18
Tasks		a	b			c	d	e	f			g						

Partner, when you show you are passionate about your work and present ideas and data, you are on your way to success. You can refer to the worksheets in Secret # 5 for the plans you wrote. Now think and write your principal and mini tasks and the date you wish to accomplish them on the timeline chart. You can refer to the "*Timeline*" number line chart in Part 1 Secret # 6 for additional guidance.

Timeline

1. Principal Task:

Date to be accomplished

a. Mini Task:

Date to be accomplished

b. Mini Task:

Date to be accomplished

c. Mini Task

Date to be accomplished

d. Mini Task

Date to be accomplished

Months 1 2 3 4 5 6 7 8 9 10 11 12 13 14 15 16 17 18
Tasks

Fantastic! You have created your timeline. Partner, begin doing all of the mini tasks you wrote on your timeline. Start accomplishing your mini task, and career objectives. At this phase you should be feeling great! Continue to observe the attitude of co-workers, and receive feedback from staff as you complete these tasks. If you feel you need to add more tasks, then do so.

Partner, you will begin to feel confident and start to acknowledge that your dreams are beginning to materialize. When all of the mini tasks are achieved, you should feel ready to accomplish your final objective. You will be able to ask the boss for a raise or to consider you for a new position. What about this? The boss offers you the position you wanted or creates one based on your special skills; and you did not even have to ask. Wouldn't that be great? Partner, my last suggestion is for you to look at yourself in the mirror and practice what you want to say to your boss at least a day prior to the big day.

Secret #7: You Have Arrived! Now Live Your Dreams!

You re-imagined your life, made a few plans, stuck to it, and elevated your ability to excel at job responsibilities. Now seek that position/endeavor. You should feel great. It's time to sing, shout or do a happy dance because you made your dreams a reality.

Congratulations, action-taker, you did it! You elevated your job skills and chances for success. Now it is time to reap the benefits. You can pat yourself on the back for a job well done.

Dreaming of something you want to accomplish is good – Achieving the dreams – PRICELESS!

You did it! You pursued your dreams. You accomplished the objectives you felt were necessary for positive career development. Even if you do not receive rewards from your boss, you should feel a sense of self fulfillment because you experienced taking on a principal task that you originally felt uncomfortable doing. Most important, you did what you set out to do. Therefore you were very successful.

At this stage, if you did not receive the offer you feel you deserve, you have options you can explore. Remember I am your partner. I can assist you while you are on your mission to advance your career, regardless of the directions you take. One option is to remain at your present job, knowing you have grown much since the beginning of your journey. In this case you would continue doing the great work you are presently doing until you receive your recognition. Another option is that you could consider seeking another job, especially now that you have a new set of job skills and mind set. Or you may want to consider starting your own business. Keep in mind that all of the options are good ones. It is just a matter of which one seems better suited for you at this stage in your life. One way or another, you win; you have obtained some awesome job-related skills.

Partner, when you have time, please reflect on the process you used to help you to accomplish your goals. Think about the beginning when you were pondering on your life's problems — up to and including your positive end results. The reflection will assist you when you are ready to take on your next challenge. Please write your last set of responses on the "*You Did It!*" page and answer the questions in the "Self-discovery Checkpoint." In the meantime, marvel on your success. Once again, congratulations.

You Did It!

1. What did you accomplish?

2. What did you learn about yourself?

3. How do you feel?

Secret # 7: You Have Arrived! Now Live Your Dreams!

SELF-DISCOVERY CHECKPOINT:

During the time we spent together you did a few Self-discovery Checks. We focused on your strengths, your life's problems, envisioned, created goals, made a timeline; and you did what you set out to do. Let's find out how you are feeling right now. So answer these questions for the last time very truthfully.

STRESS LEVEL ASSESSMENT

1. **What is your present stress level from 1 through 10? Please circle your response.**

(1 = very low stress level, 5 = some stress, 10 = very high stress level).

Stress Number Line

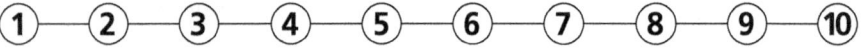

2. **What stresses are you experiencing right now, if any? Explain.**

3. **Based on the Stress vs. Success balance beams:**

    i. Which of the 3 diagrams best represents you?

    a. Stress is overpowering

    b. I can succeed/ Success is possible

    c. Balanced

    ii. Which diagram best describes how you feel when you are working at your job?

    a. Stress is overpowering

    b. I can succeed/ Success is possible

    c. Balanced

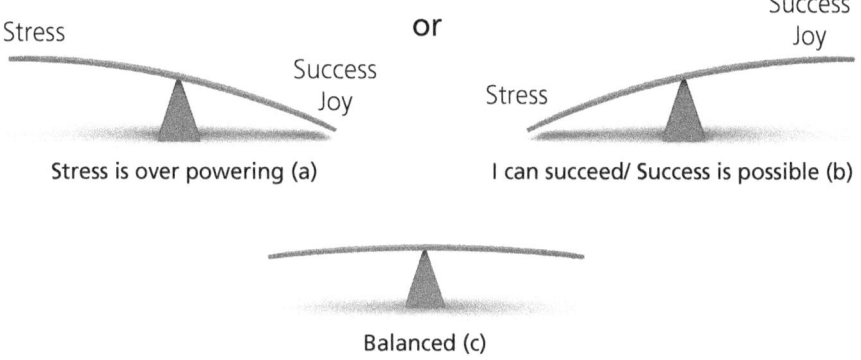

Secret # 7: You Have Arrived! Now Live Your Dreams!

4. **Do you feel you can achieve success in the near future?**
   Yes ___ No ___

   i. If yes, in what ways do you feel you can be successful?

   ii. If no, why not?

5. **How would you rank your energy level on a scale of 1 through 10? Please circle your response.**

   (1= very low, 5= some energy, 10= very high)

   Energy Level Number Line

   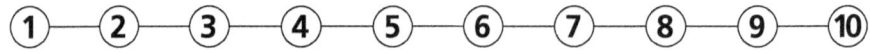

   Your self-discovery check results should be great, especially since you completed your tasks and had success. Feel proud!

Part 4

Especially for Older Adults

"The road not taken..."

Robert Frost

Especially for Older Adults

This section of the book is devoted to people who are sixty and older and are no longer working. Now might be a great time to consider doing things you have on your 'must-do' list. Younger adults may want to venture into some of the exercises and worksheets presented in this part of the book in order to be more fulfilled in their lives as well. You are more than welcomed to read *Especially for Older Adults*.

Many older adults have raised children. Many senior citizens have grandchildren. Some have great-grandchildren and great-great-grandchildren. Isn't it wonderful to be alive and spend time with members of your family tree? Wouldn't it be great for you to enjoy yourself even at this stage in your life?

Children, adults and other seniors observe senior citizens. They observe how you act, move, and behave. There are young people who think being a senior citizen is a painful reality, while others think of it as just another stage in life. When you are around younger people how do they respond to you? Do they say they want to live a life similar to yours when they reach your age? Or do they express and show empathy when they are around you? How do you want to be perceived in the eyes of people younger than you? Do you want to be thought of as someone who is enjoying life to the fullest, or someone hoping, or not hoping, to survive until the next day?

If you are a great-grandparent or great-great-grandparent and you are living an independent healthy lifestyle that is fantastic! I know a few women in their nineties who take public transportation by themselves in New York City, sing, dance and are good at voicing their opinions. I aspire to be as healthy and independent as they are in my later years.

Now let's talk about you. You may have been involved in raising children or working for many years. Do you think it is time to give some thought to self? I am not suggesting that you give up the responsibilities you presently have. Do you plan to wait until you are in your nineties to accomplish your dreams? Do you have a 'must-do' list that serves only as a conversation piece when you are amongst friends and family?

If you feel it is your time to treat yourself to what life has to offer, then I will guide you on your journey. I want you to enjoy this stage in your life. Make it wonderful. Be a role model for younger family members, friends and acquaintances. Allow them to think of you as an older adult who is enjoying life to the fullest. This could inspire them to do the same when they are your age.

I know many older adults have aches, pains and medical conditions. You may be saying your health plays a role in deciding what you can do; however, if you are eager enough, in most cases you can find a way. I know some people who are physically challenged who are doing some remarkable things. There are people who have artificial legs who participate in races. Do not let the challenge rule you. You become the greatest of role models when you face your challenges and continue on your quest for success. So please do not sit at home moping and acting incapable of doing anything. There are things you can do to enjoy your life.

For those of you who may not have sufficient funds, sometimes your children or other people offer money. Some people put dollars away and in a short period of time they have saved the money needed to accomplish their goals. So please do not think everything is impossible.

If you have good health and the money, you are blessed. You can be on your way to a good time as well as have the ability to do other great things in your life. As a reminder, please consult with your doctor to discuss your medical condition and any possible immunizations. Also consult your financial advisor about decisions regarding money.

So let's move you along on your journey of fun and adventure, and begin by reminiscing about all of the things you have accomplished in your life. You will be asked to record information in worksheets or you can ask a younger person to write what you state to him/her. The recorder can learn much about your life and what you accomplished. Talking about your wonderful past experiences can be a nice way to bond with the person who is writing for you. Are you ready to begin? Great!

I want you to think about some of the wonderful things you have done and have achieved in your life. For example, were you engaged in community service, engaged in sports, performed in shows, won special awards? Let's focus your attention on the *"Young Achiever"* worksheet that follows. I would like you to reminisce about the wonderful things you have accomplished. Think of your childhood years up to the age of 18. Once again, as a youngster, what have you done and accomplished? Think positively. Write about those positive achievements.

Young Achiever

1.

2.

3.

4.

5.

Especially for Older Adults

Now that you have written about your youthful years, I would like you to focus on your adult years. However, I want you to think about all of your accomplishments up to age 59. I have provided the "Adult Achiever" worksheet for you. This consists of two parts. The first part asks you what you have done for "Other People." The second section asks you to record what you have achieved for "Self."

So let's start with *"Other People."* Did you spend time raising children as opposed to going to work? Did you help your loved one, who is not physically able to do for himself/herself? Did you volunteer time at soup kitchens and shelters? Were you on committees to help improve your neighborhood? Did you donate blood or body organs? Think about the wonderful things you have done for other people and write your responses in the *"Adult Achiever − Other People"* worksheet.

Adult Achiever – Other People

1.

2.

3.

4.

5.

Especially for Older Adults

You should feel proud of yourself. You helped others. You care. Now on the next worksheet, which is *"Adult Achiever-Self,"* I would like you to first think about the wonderful things you accomplished for yourself prior to age 60. For example, did you earn a higher educational degree, create an artwork that gave you special recognition, perform in a show/concert, win a special award, start your own business, write a book, buy your own house or car? Did you visit a foreign country, get married, have children? Did you bungee jump or see your favorite star perform in person? There is something else I would like you to include: how did you feel before, during and after each experience? Now have fun writing, or have someone write down all the wonderful things you did on the *"Adult Achiever-Self"* list.

Don't you feel fantastic knowing you have done some things in your life that have made you feel happy? Spend a few moments cherishing those fond memories. Why not put a smile on your face while you are reminiscing about your accomplishments.

Adult Achiever - Self

1.

2.

3.

4.

5.

Especially for Older Adults

These are the wonderful things that make you a dynamic person. Is there anything else you would like to add to any of these worksheets? Please feel free to brag about your accomplishments while you are writing. The more you add, the better. I want you to feel proud of yourself and know you have earned the right to live your dreams. Why? Because you deserve it. Also, with the positive thoughts you are probably feeling right now you may want to accomplish more. Your past accomplishments indicate you were successful in whatever you set out to do.

This next section is devoted to helping you to enjoy your senior years. Remember, you are not waiting until you are in your nineties to have fun. So let's update your activities list, or add new objectives. Hopefully you are feeling inspired and excited at this point. You have me to coach you through the process of fulfilling your life during your senior years. I am excited about the next list you will create. Are you? So let's continue the journey.

Since you finished writing your list of things you have already done, review the list one more time to see if there is anything else you want to add. Look at the 'before, during and after comments' you wrote. Does anything appear consistent? For example, did you seem to have the same general feeling when you accomplished something? I am asking you to review the list because this may be a way to inspire you to want to do a few more wonderful things in your life for yourself and for others.

Now that you have written your prior accomplishments and what you have already done on your list, we are going to take a power break. I want you to stop for a few moments. Smile. Let's take a few deep breaths. Deep breath, inhale; now exhale. Once again inhale, now exhale. You may want to drink a sip of some cool refreshing water or a hot, minty, herbal tea. Also, you may want to stand up and stretch your legs. Are you ready to continue? Great!

I want to share a story about a single woman in her eighties I met while on a tour in Cambodia. The ancient sites we visited necessitated walking on rugged, underdeveloped ground, and the woman knew to hire an escort to help her move around. She obtained personal assistance and devices such as a walking stick and a wheelchair. She rarely used either of the devices, but both devices were available. It was obvious that this woman did not want to miss out on one of her 'must do' adventures. She did not allow her age to stop her from visiting a foreign country.

Here is a story about another woman I knew. This ninety-two-year-old woman asked me if I wanted to go on a safari in East Africa with her. Yes, you read that correctly. She was ninety-two. She was active and did not use a cane. I want to share with you how physically fit she was. We went on a trip to one of the Six Flags amusement parks and she was able to keep up with the youthful group as we walked throughout the park. In addition, she was flirting with some of the men along the way! I enjoyed being in her company. I hope to live as long as her and be as healthy as she was.

I feel this is a good time to share the following information. I have spoken with several older adults who have expressed a desire to go on a cruise. However, their partner did not want to travel via a cruise. As a result none of these couples have cruised. In most cases the reason why their partner did not want to cruise was because they were concerned about possibly experiencing motion sickness. I have a suggestion for you if you have this type of situation. Maybe a riverboat cruise could be the answer for you and your partner. You can spend weeks on a riverboat cruise. I can attest that people on this type of boat do not experience nearly as much rocking as on a cruise ship. Your meals, entertainment and sightseeing in another land usually make a lovely, unforgettable experience. You can choose a riverboat cruise that takes up to thirty passengers, or one that allows hundreds of passengers. Your choice. Ask your doctor about cruising.

So now I have a few questions for you. What would you like to accomplish? And what has kept you from achieving your dreams? Have you had a dream since childhood that you have not accomplished yet? When was the last time you accomplished something? And when was the last time you felt fulfilled? Maybe your response to the first question needs to be on your 'must do' list.

Before you create your 'must do' list, I would like you to spend a little bit of time envisioning what you want to do. You want to continue to be fulfilled and enjoy as much of your life as possible, yes? We will begin the envisioning process. Let's take a deep breath, breathe in, and breathe out. Once again breathe in, now breathe out.

Partner, *re-imagine your life*. I want you to imagine yourself in the place you want to be. Who is with you; or are you alone? What are you doing? What are you wearing? Is acquiring better health important to you? Do you see yourself walking more or engaging in some form of exercise a few days per week? Do you see yourself at a club, organization or social gathering? How are you feeling before, during and after the adventure or task you are imagining?

I would like you to envision this thought. When you were a child and had no money, did you participate in fun-filled games and activities that made you laugh so hard your body was hurting? Partner, I don't want you to be in pain, but I think you understand my point — contentment, happiness. Why not indulge in some of those activities with friends or family? For instance, you can have fun singing, dancing and playing games with family and friends.

    This is a good time to talk about you generating a *"Must Do"* list. Let's call your *"Must Do"* list goals you wish to accomplish. What do you want to achieve within a year or two? You may want to consider prioritizing your list by asking yourself which goal seems the most fulfilling to accomplish? What I mean is which goals will make you feel the most content? Some activities can be done immediately, while other activities/tasks may take longer to achieve. Can you do another task/activity while working on the one that may take more time to accomplish? If one goal may take a year to accomplish, while another one may take only two months, you can accomplish the goal that will take the least amount of time first, along with any other ones that can be done immediately and still work on the longer-term goal. Please look at the *"Must Do"* worksheet on the page that follows for one moment. While you are reminiscing about the questions I just asked you and the sort of things you would like to do, close your eyes. After you open your eyes, record your responses and thoughts on the *"Must Do"* worksheet. I would like you to write a few tasks/activities on your list and why you chose them; please indicate an approximate date by which you plan to accomplish the goals.

Must Do

1. Activity/Task:

Reason for wanting to do activity/task:

Approximate date to do task:

2. Activity/Task:

Reason for wanting to do activity/task:

Approximate date to do task:

3. Activity/Task:

Reason for wanting to do activity/task:

Approximate date to do task:

You may be saying, "Rosa, I have responsibilities. I just cannot go off into the sunset and leave my responsibilities behind." Then I have a question for you. What are those things that are preventing you from accomplishing your dreams? Partner, usually there are ways to manage a situation, especially if you know you want to do a particular task or activity. Communicate, communicate, communicate! Express to family and/or your doctor how important personal satisfaction and fulfillment is to you. You can show them the list you wrote which indicates your reason for wanting to do a specific task or activity. Another suggestion would be to give plenty of notice to people who rely on you so that they can make necessary arrangements.

Isn't this fantastic! You imagined what you want to do and wrote it down with a tentative date in mind. You are so close to making this dream become a reality. You must prepare yourself for your first activity on your *"Must Do"* worksheet. Who do you need to contact in addition to the people who rely on you? If you want to consider going on a cruise, safari or any other type of adventure, speak with your partner, doctor and travel agent. Do you have pets that need to be taken care of? Do you need assistance from financial advisors, mentors, etc. in order to fulfill your goals? Start as soon as possible and take care of whatever you need to do in order to check off the activity/task on your *"Must Do"* list. Both of you or just you, if you are single, may discover it is time to begin a new set of adventures.

As a final note for all of you that believe in God, maybe you want to thank God for allowing you to be able to accomplish what you have done in the past, and that you are alive and able to create your new list with more fulfillment, enjoyment and excitement on the way.

A Final Word

I have devoted this book to helping adults who face challenges in their personal and professional lives. In all four parts of the book I ask you, the reader, to think back to when you were a youngster. Our childhood years play a significant role in how we handle situations and how we turn out as adults. So my final word to all who have children or work with children is this:

Please provide as many positive experiences as possible to children. Love them, enjoy them, and compliment them often so their journey to success can be a smooth one.

About the Author

Rosa Yordan is a certified professional life coach, mentor and crisis intervention leader who has assisted thousands of people in their personal and professional dilemmas. She has made numerous television appearances on telethons. Rosa has written and implemented proposals to aid people in crises abroad and in the U.S.A. In addition, she has written proposals and instructed hundreds of educators and parents who interact with children who possess behavioral management issues. Rosa is the author of the fairy tale "The Disabled Prince" with a potent message for children of all ages. The book's message is that regardless of your emotional or physical challenge, you can accomplish your goals.

Rosa has a Bachelor's degree in Speech Pathology and Audiology and minored in Cultural Anthropology at Herbert. H. Lehman College, CUNY. She received a Master's degree in Special Education – Emotionally Handicapping Conditions at Lehman College. Rosa's job awarded her a scholarship; earning her a Master's degree in Supervision and Administration at Bank Street College in N.Y.C.

Rosa Yordan is Founder and CEO of Transformation+ Inc., a life coaching service that is based in New York. Transformation+ Inc. offers workshops and one-on-one coaching sessions. We are available to guide you towards your professional and personal successes based on your vision. In addition we offer Re-Imagine Your Life events for just one day - featuring events such as high teas, masquerade balls, roaring twenties, game shows, fund raisers and many other wonderful events.

www.ingramcontent.com/pod-product-compliance
Lightning Source LLC
Chambersburg PA
CBHW032044150426
43194CB00006B/410